JEWEL

Deeper Aspects of Hinduism

MUMTAZ ALI

Compiled by

A. MENON

with a foreword by

KARAN SINGH

A Sterling Paperback

STERLING PAPERBACKS
An imprint of
Sterling Publishers (P) Ltd.
A-59 Okhla Industrial Area, Phase-II,
New Delhi-110020.
Tel : 6313023, 6916209, 6916169
E-mail: ghai@nde.vsnl.net.in
www.sterlingpublishers.com

ISBN 81 207 2046 6
Reprint 1998, 2001

Published by Sterling Publishers Pvt. Ltd., New Delhi-110 016.
Lasertypeset by Vikas Compographics, New Delhi.
Printed at Prolific Incorporated, New Delhi-110020.
Cover design by Rattan Razdan

CONTENTS

Foreword by Karan Singh v

1. The Mystique of 'M' : A Profile 1
2. Towards Greater Glory and a Happier Life 24
3. Thus Spake the Master 43
4. The Essence of Hinduism 86
5. Illusions Under which We Live 99
6. Vedantic Quest for the True Self 114
7. In the World but not of the World 130
8. The Gayatri Mantra 142
9. Misconceptions About Kundalini 151
10. Fear of Death 157
11. Pain in the Light of Yoga 160

FOREWORD

Hinduism is a many-splendoured and multi-faceted edifice, containing and reflecting an endless array of possibilities for spiritual growth and integration. Based essentially upon the sublime teachings of the *Upanishads*, the secret of Hinduism's continued vitality down through the long and tortuous corridors of time, despite repeated invasions and repression, lies in its capacity for creative reinterpretation. Indeed, the whole history of Hinduism can be viewed as a series of challenge and creative response, a process which continues down to the present day. In the emerging global society it is my conviction that the universal principles of Hinduism are becoming increasingly relevant as we hurtle headlong into the third millennium A.D. astride the irreversible arrow of time.

Theoretical formulations apart, Hinduism involves treading a spiritual path, and there are many. It is these individual pathways involving a creative interaction between the Guru and the disciple that provide the circulatory life-blood of Hinduism, making it a powerful vehicle for inner growth and spiritual realisation. In this context the experience of individuals who have trodden the path is of great value. The present book *Jewel in the Lotus* revolves around the life experience and teachings of Mumtaz Ali, better known as 'M'. Some may find it surprising that a person born a Muslim should have such a deep insight into and experience with the Hindu tradition, but the real spiritual path knows no boundary of race or religion, sex or creed, language or nationality. And the mystics of all the world's great religions — the Rishis, the Siddhas, the Tirthankaras, the Bodhisattvas, the Sufis, the Gurus and the saints have all illuminated one or other facets of the immeasurable resplendence of the Divine.

I have had occasion to know 'M' over the last few years, and we have spoken together on several occasions including a three-day workshop on the *Kena Upanishad* over which I presided. He combines an excellent grasp of the *Upanishadic* teachings with deep insight into the heart of the spiritual tradition based on his own remarkable experiences. This book in which he has dealt with some of the deeper aspects of Hinduism will, I am sure, be of great interest to students of contemporary religion, as well as seekers for truth around the world.

Vijaya Dashami
11 October 1997

Karan Singh

1

THE MYSTIQUE OF 'M'

A Profile

"Guru Maharaj had put to sleep many agitated souls. Thousands of people had listened to him and found great peace in a world torn by tension and strife. He had lectured for years on how to relax the body and the mind without the use of drugs but no one knew the number of sleepless nights he would have had to spend if it was not for the great saviour of mankind—the sleeping pill.

Five minutes after he had drained a glass of water to wash down the tablets, he was fast asleep, blissfully deep asleep, the nearest thing to *nirvana.*"

Thus ends the story "The Saviour" published some years ago in the Sunday edition of a national newspaper. The story is about a much revered and feted holy man who has been the saviour of many who flock to him for succour, and ironically where he finds it himself. It might look like a tongue-in-cheek comment or satire on the many self-styled, or a la R.K. Narayan's *The Guide*, unwillingly promoted gurus of today. Ergo, it could have come only from the vitriolic pen of either a sceptic all out to run down spirituality or a disgruntled follower of a particular guru.

In the event, the writer is neither. He is Mumtaz Ali, popularly known as M, who has been a spiritual seeker since his childhood and who has spent a major part of the 47 years of his life till now with many genuine spiritual masters. In his own right, he has been, for the past few years, a spiritual guide to an ever-increasing number of people whom he regards as his friends and not credulous devotees or disciples.

Considering that this story was written years ago long before he embarked upon his present mission of sharing his spiritual experience and wisdom with others, is he not likely to regret or recant the theme of the story from his own pen?

No, not likely. If he appeared to cock a snook at the guru culture then, he continues to do so now; but his trenchant comment is not against gurus in toto. He is only against the operation of Gresham's Law ('Bad money drives out good') in the spiritual field, the fake gurus outnumbering the genuine.

Here, a question might be raised: Who is Mumtaz Ali to sit in judgment on the authenticity or falsity of a guru and, even if he is right in general, what is his own provenance, his credentials? The answer may be found in the following thumbnail sketch of his life.

Is he a guru, a sage, a realised master, a philosopher? None of these or all of them in a happy combination? Ask him and in answer you get an ambivalent shrug of his shoulders and a cryptic admonition tendered—and tempered—with a disarming smile: "You decide for yourself who I should be to you."

Perhaps, a faint clue as to what he considers to be himself can be inferred from his wholehearted endorsement of the *Rig*[1]*Vedic* lines given below:

The source from which this universe has risen
And whether it was made or uncreated,
He only knows from the highest heaven who
Rules, the all-seeing Lord—or does he not know?

Mumtaz Ali says, "Admittedly, this vedic hymn seeks the dizzy heights of speculative philosophy; but the mind of its originator, unlike that of the weak, faith-blinded disciples of many a present-day guru or godman (who demands absolute surrender of all intellectual and critical faculties), bristled with doubt and scepticism—the most essential qualities which any true seeker of truth, any scientific investigator, no matter in what field, must possess."

As his tacit appreciation of the hymn suggests, he is a seeker who has no desire to sacrifice his intellectual and critical faculties in his spiritual quest. Nor is he an iconoclast in the mould of J. Krishnamurti as some who meet Mumtaz Ali first take him to be; such a view would be wholly invidious to both, and therefore, unfounded. Unlike Krishnamurti, Mumtaz Ali has abiding and experientially validated faith in the spiritual wisdom of all scriptures, not because of the sacrosanct authority ascribed to them but because of his personal insight into that wisdom gained from years of spiritual practices. Again, his acceptance and propagation of the spiritual wisdom is in character with his acknowledgement of a guru; quite a contrary view from that of Krishnamurti.

If at all he can be compared to anyone, it can only be, very loosely at that, to a member of the Hasidic sect. Like them[2] he too believes that by virtue of being an early pilgrim than his contemporaries in the dense spiritual forest, he may be able to help others—by pointing out a thicket here, a marsh there—to avoid the unknown snares that impede the journey out towards the clear light of spiritual wisdom. He may also, as he would say, show the probable path that he has, intuitively and through experience, found for himself. No more. The rest, the ultimate goal, depends on the seeker himself. All he can do is to show[3] the man himself as he really is and to help him to develop his real, inner self, his permanent part.

All in all, any conventional approach to force-fit him into a stereotype is futile. If external symbols alone are sufficient to evaluate a person, then he can be described as a fairly well-off (a car and a decent house) householder with a teacher-wife and two children, sophisticatedly modern in appearance and behaviour, well-groomed silvery hair, clean-shaven face, dressed in socially acceptable conventions—in short, a man who has *savoir vivre*—and finally, a Muslim by birth, who is as much at home in the *Quran* as in the Hindu scriptures and the *Bible*. None of these can, individually or even collectively, mark him out to be any different; even his profound knowledge of scriptures other than his own does not invest him uniqueness—catholicism in scriptural scholarship is almost commonplace. There are many others of different persuasions who are equally scholarly, if not more.

Then, where lies the difference? Perhaps the only expression that can come closer to describing his charisma is the French expression *je ne sais quoi,* an indefinable something. Having said that, one retreats from further exploration into the mystique that is Mumtaz Ali, or as he personally prefers to be called, 'M'. If there is, in this preference, an attempt at emulating Franz Kafka whose protagonist K in the novel, *The Trial*, is so anonymous and mysterious as to defeat any deterministic slotting, it is not in M conscious or discernible. Nor is he appropriating for himself the fame of the great chronicler of Sri Ramakrishna Paramahamsa's life, M. Nor is it a wish to relinquish his name, Mumtaz, whose gender bias is obvious—in fact, he is not ashamed of it and he may even tell you about the hilarious consequences that his name evoked in the life of a couple of his married friends. His choice is another way of self-effacement that he exhibits in his various unobtrusive actions. To parody Gertrude Stein of "A rose is a rose" fame, M is M and it is by that letter that he will be referred to in the rest of this sketch.

M was born in a moderately affluent and educated Deccani Muslim family in the capital of Kerala,

Thiruvananthapuram. He had, along with his two sisters younger than he, an ordinary childhood. Like any other child of his age, he too was fond of listening to stories and his grandmother indulged him in his love. As is to be expected from a devout Muslim lady, the stories were of the Prophet Mohammed and saints of that religion. Since he had not shown any precocity, either intellectually or spiritually, what kind of impact these stories had on him, no one can say—not even M himself. Nevertheless, as later events were to prove, they must have notched, albeit subliminally, some mark on his young, impressionable mind. Whatever be the reason, he was formed into the ready receptacle (*upadhi*) for the experience that was to come soon—an experience that is, in the light of hindsight, epiphanic in its import.

M was about eight years old at that time. He had come back home after his evening games and was in the backyard of the house readying himself to obey the standing order that he should enter the house only after washing the dirt of the playground off his person. The golden spangles of the sun were stippling the dusk with fast changing shadowy forms and figures. His eyes followed the interesting chiaroscuro with childish enjoyment. Soon, his eyes found a form more substantial and static than the fleeting shadows. This was under a big jackfruit tree. Its solidity riveted his attention. It started moving towards him. As it approached nearer and nearer, he could make it out to be that of a man of flesh and blood and no mere phantom of his imagination. The boy stood transfixed to the spot, unable to move; he was by now in the grip of an emotion which was a mixture of awe, curiosity and sheer fascination. ("Normally, as a child I should have been afraid of a stranger appearing before me, but, incomprehensibly, I was not." M recalled years later when he thought and talked about it.)

The man slowly walked towards the boy. The stranger wore a single, white loin-cloth (*mundu* in

Malayalam), and he had long hair and a straggly beard. He tenderly laid his hand on M and spoke to him in Deccani Urdu, the boy's mother tongue: "I am your teacher, though you won't be meeting me for a long time to come. But I shall always be there, overseeing your growth. You are very young now; so continue with your normal schooling. From time to time, you will, of course, come by a different kind of knowledge." After enjoining the dazed boy to strict silence about the 'visitation' till the time was ripe for its revelation, the stranger walked away or disappeared all of a sudden. Though his young brain was unable to make any sense out of the words spoken to him or of the stranger (in his childish ignorance, how was he to know or recognise this most important person in his life?), he decided to remain silent about this incident. Not that he remembered making any covenant with the stranger about keeping the visit a secret; but, for some inexplicable reason, he wanted to hold on to it as a privately cherished secret.

What is of significance is that his life took a different direction from then on. He began to be drawn more and more towards pursuits which, considering his age, could be labelled aberrant or deviant. Outwardly, he didn't appear to be much different from his coevals, except for his penchant for things spiritual and for frequently withdrawing himself into a mental shell of his own.

Time and the immediate life around him began inevitably to drop the curtain on that dramatic encounter at dusk. Two years had passed. And now, as if to jog his memory, an incident occurred which was indirectly prophetic of the words spoken by the stranger. M was playing 'hide and seek' with his friends. Suddenly, he felt that his breath was suspended, and strangely, it was not causing him discomfort like that of one gasping for breath. On the contrary, he became inexplicably blissful. After some time, his breathing became normal. Later, he could identify his experience by the yogic term *keval kumbhak.*[4] The bliss he experienced for that short spell opened to him a world that he never knew existed. (After this experience, he has been able to will himself into this state with what he calls a 'sigh'. Or, is it the Sufi mystic's *mantra* 'suriuff'?)

Unknown to, unrealised by him, his promised 'education' had begun. He became more and more attracted to scriptures of all kinds—his love for them remains Catholic even now. He also became a regular at any congregation that was religious, spiritual or philosophical in intent.

When he was around thirteen, he would go one evening to the house of one Pillai, whose nephew tutored M in mathematics. During one of his visits, there he met a man of venerable appearance of some sixty summers past. Despite the close-cropped, silvery grey hair, a sure sign of a man past his prime, he was vibrant with the health and physique of a youth. Wearing a short-sleeved shirt and typical Kerala *mundu*, he was sitting cross-legged on a bench. The smell of incense pervaded the room. The gentleman addressed him in Malayalam, perhaps, sensing the shyness of the boy, "Come, come near." M walked up to him, hesitantly. He was wondering what the man wanted with him. As it turned out, he was in for another strange experience. The old man first patted him on the back and then caressed his neck and head as if in inspection. After this strange action, he muttered more to himself than to M. "Umm... good! Everything will be all right in good time." Unfathomably, M was again transported to that breathless condition of ineffable bliss! He was awestricken and tongue-tied; without a word to anyone he went straight home.

He was not even curious to know who that man was, such was his altered state of mind.

The next day, 'M' learned the name of the man who was one of the many souls he was to meet on his spiritual journey. He was not well-known; he was known as Pujapura Swami since he was living in a place of that name in Thiruvananthapuram. Before the reverential appellation accrued to him, he had worked as a clerk in the Accountant General's office until retirement. In his youth, he had been initiated into Vedantic practices by a great teacher; and ever since, he had led an exemplary life of the spirit, absorbed in a bliss that surpasses ordinary understanding; all the while performing his duties like an ordinary man. Though a householder, he was considered a self-realised soul by all who came to know him. What can be a greater avowal of the Swami's spiritual credentials than the attendance, although infrequent, at this householder's *satsangs* of a great *sannyasin* who had even renounced his loin cloth and who was averse even to the whiff of worldly life?

M was barely fortunate to have met the Pujapura Swami, for soon the Swami attained *samadhi*. A few years later, however, when M was about seventeen, he chanced upon a compilation of the Swami's teachings, courtesy a friend, which was in private circulation. It contained the essence of Vedanta in very simple language.

By then, M was more than convinced that it was not a mere overworked fancy that magicked the stranger into being some years ago. Weren't the subsequent events proof enough of the authenticity of that experience? How else could one explain the way in which he came by spiritual knowledge, as if fortuitously? Or, to risk a bit of levity, was it the case of the mountain coming to Mohammed? It was not that he was an unwilling adept, but, given the religious persuasion he was heir to by birth—however unorthodox his immediate family was—it would not have been easy for him to indulge in pursuits that would certainly have dubbed him an apostate. (Interestingly, he learned about yoga from a book his father borrowed from a friend. This book was B.K.S. Iyengar's *Light on Yoga*).

M's spiritual adventure was not merely intellectual. He was rigorously trained in *ashtanga* yoga by a yoga teacher of repute near his place, Shri Sharma. A *tantric* instructed him in certain *mantras* and lent him Arthur Avalon's *Serpent Power*. He also read Swami Chinmayananda's *Japa Yoga and Gayatri* and began to chant the *Gayatri Mantra* regularly. His appetite for knowledge was voracious. He befriended the librarian at the Public Library in Thiruvananthapuram and this helped in ensuring a steady supply of books. Books and books and more books; he devoured them all—the *Upanishads*, the different *Gitas*, Yoga and Vedanta texts. His reading had a gratuitous outcome; he discovered that Sanskrit was none too difficult to learn; and he did learn it. It was a necessary means to first-hand comprehension of the Hindu scriptures.

However, he did not limit his quest to the cold print of books and often unaided practices. Sufficiently early in his life, he realised that there was no substitute for learning from the living masters. Underlying this realisation must have been an inchoate feeling. A prophecy had to be fulfilled. Wasn't he told by that stranger under the jackfruit tree that he would meet him again? Perhaps it was the hope of meeting him again that propelled him towards many spiritual leaders of that time. Who knew in what form the stranger would condescend to meet him again?

One of the masters whom he sought out was Swami Tapasyananda, a direct disciple of Swami Shivananda (Mahapurushji Maharaj); the Swamiji was then the head of the Ramakrishna Mission in Thiruvananthapuram. Soon after, he met Chempazhanti Swami. At that time M was among the first batch of students in the first Loyola Junior College that the Jesuits had started at Sreekaryam in Thiruvananthapuram. The Swami was living in a village a few kilometres away from

Sreekaryam-Chempazhanti, the birthplace of Sri Narayana Guru, the great reformer-saint of Kerala.

Chempazhanti Swami was a teashop owner before people began to regard him as a saint. He was a great devotee of Sri Rama and the local belief had it that he emulated the monkey god, Hanuman; for a long time he lived on nuts and fruits, virtually living in and on trees.

When M met Chempazhanti Swami, the Swami was living in Chenkottukonam near Chempazhanti. He was emaciated, frail and extremely delicate looking; a captivating smile wreathed his pinched face under a huge crown of coiled-up matted hair. Taking a pinch of ash, he touched M's forehead with it. He asked M to open his mouth. A surprised M complied and into his open mouth the Swami dropped a couple of grapes and said, "Needs to ripen; will ripen. Learn *bhajans*." (The Swami was greatly fond of *bhajans* and *keertans.*) Was he referring to the grapes, this irreverent thought was about to fleet through M's mind before he killed it. The import of the injunction struck him. He sat in the holy presence for a while and meditated before leaving the place.

In those days, M had a close Brahmin friend whose father was an ardent devotee of the Sai Baba of Shirdi. M happened to see a picture of the Baba at his friend's place and he had an immediate and irresistible urge to know more of the Baba's life. That was all he needed—the urge; the very next day, an advocate who was his friend's landlord lent him a copy of the *Life of Sai Baba of Shirdi* by Narasimhaswami. From the same source, he obtained *Sai Sat Charita.* And, inevitably M was attracted to the life and teachings of the great *fakir*.

Once the adept is ready, things begin to happen. M's life is a prime example of how true this is.

From a friend, who was then a medical student and is now a neuro-surgeon, he heard about a woman *avadhuta*, called Maayi Ma. She lived on the beaches of

Kanyakumari; no one knew where she hailed from or what language she spoke. The locals thought she was over a hundred years old.

Curiosity, tinged with spiritual fervour, sent M to her. Alone, he reached Kanyakumari, which is not very far from Thiruvananthapuram, by bus. Now the problem was to meet Maayi Ma. "Where would you look for one who doesn't have a permanent abode?" M was wondering, when a young man accosted him and said, "If you want to meet Maayi Ma, she is near the entrance to the Devi Temple on the beach." Lest he should miss her, M almost ran towards the spot, climbing over a wall, hopping over the rocky beach. And there she was. A woman who looked to be in her sixties. She was stark-naked. Her facial features had something of a Bengali in them; or at least, that was what M surmised.

She sat on a rock, a circle of street dogs forming, as it were, a security ring around her. The dogs snarled at him when he drew closer. He stopped in his tracks. Maayi Ma looked at him; her whole face broke into a beatific smile, her eyes atwinkle with an ageless light. As she motioned M to come near her, she sent the dogs scampering away by apparently scolding them in a language that sounded like Bengali. The dogs moved away and sat at a distance, still maintaining a sort of vigil on the stranger.

M sat down on a rock. She noticed the bunch of bananas he had with him. She told him something in that same strange language the drift of which M completely missed. Perhaps, she was asking for the bananas. Anyway he had bought them for her and he offered them to her. She plucked a few and threw them to the dogs, ate two herself and returned the rest to M. He was not sure what spiritual protocol he had to observe with a person like this. All he could think of doing was to sit there with closed eyes and try tuning in with this odd soul and her ambience. How long he sat there, he did not know. When he opened his eyes she was still there. Again she vouchsafed him a smile even far brighter than the earlier one. Now she said, *'Jao, jao, Theek....'* The last words were a murmur of incomprehensible sounds. When *paramahansas* ask you to go, one has no business to tarry. Yes, M had no doubt of the authenticity of her identity, despite all the external evidence to the contrary, evidence that normally would consign her to the asylum. M's own spiritual evolution could help him intuit her greatness. After prostrating to her, M returned to Thiruvananthapuram.

The following morning, he discovered through another strange experience that his intuition did not betray him.

After long hours of meditation the previous night, M was sleeping late. He then had a wonderfully vivid dream. He dreamt that he was a mendicant with matted hair. Clad only in a *kaupin*, he was sitting in *padmasana*, meditating under a banyan tree that stood right in the middle of a junction where four paths met and parted. All around was a dense forest. A faint sound disturbed him in his meditation; he opened his eyes and saw Maayi Ma, now grown to Amazonian proportions, walking towards him with a stick aloft in her hand. She asked him for something to eat. Taking a couple of grains of beaten rice he had hidden in his matted hair, he gave them to her. 'Are you hungry, too ?' she asked. When he said he was, she told him, "You don't need this. Your hunger is for a different thing."

Suddenly she pressed the middle of his forehead with what he felt to be her thumb. An ocean of bliss coursed through him, from the crown of his head to the soles of his feet. Every cell of his being pulsated with it.

He woke up; or rather, he floated up into a wakeful state, but the ethereal bliss remained with him. He sat up slowly, stretched his legs. He walked towards the bathroom, he felt that he was a thistledown wafting in the air; he did not feel even his limbs moving. After some time, he regained control over his body and mind; but the stream of bliss gurgled in the core of his being. Ever since, that ineffable bliss has stayed with him—at times low, at other times high, but always there.

Many are the masters M came across on his path, but none stranger than Kaladi Mastaan, a gem among Sufis. Having already acquired some knowledge about Sufism (incidentally one of his great-uncles was a well-known Sufi), M used to attend local Sufi groups of different schools. It was in one such meeting that he heard about Kaladi Mastaan. He was told that the Mastaan lived naked on the beach near Bimapalli in Thiruvananthapuram. M went there.

When M first saw him, the Mastaan was holding a cup of tea in his hand, blissfully unaware of the derisive stares of the passersby. He smiled at M and offered him the cup after sipping it himself. He then said, "Big thief has come to steal the treasure. Take it, take it legitimately." After a prolonged silence, he lit a cigarette. After a few hard puffs, he held out the cigarette to M and commanded him to smoke. M smoked. He took it back from M again to smoke it to the end. M sat before him and meditated. Before long he was startled out of his meditation when a shower of sand trickled down on his head. The perpetrator of the outrage was none other than the Mastaan. What would have been construed as a mad man's act by others—the Mastaan was notorious in that area as a mad man to the uninitiated—M took as a blessing. And he was not far from the truth; that mad act of the Mastaan, cleared, as it were, the conduits to spiritual growth. (Though the Mastaan is gone a long time now, his tomb is visited by many even today.)

An equally weird personage M encountered was Poonthara Swami. He was not living very far from the place of the Mastaan. With his strange ways, he was also regarded as insane by the general public. M knew better; he knew that the Swami must be God-intoxicated. M, naturally, visited him. This time the blessing was in the form of a kick to M's chest. M considered it a timely kick, because it cleared in him the passage through which the mighty energy travels. Later, when M went looking for him to thank him, he had disappeared.

There is a coda to this story. While M was trying to track down Poonthara Swami, an impressive-looking man, claiming himself to be the closest disciple of the Swami, attempted to foist himself upon M. The bravura act of the charlatan did not deceive M for a moment. On the contrary, it taught him the unsavory fact that, on the spiritual path, there lurk many predators ready to pounce on the unwary and the gullible. This, M is not tired of reiterating, need not deter the genuine seeker.

When M was twenty, when others of his age were—and are—after pelf and prosperity, he decided to go to the Himalayas, a place considered *de rigueur* in the itinerary of any seeker. (The slight tongue-in-cheek levity is intentional to underscore the fact that places alone, however spiritually salubrious they are, would not be sufficient, without that deep longing for attaining the Ultimate.) En route to Hardwar, he spent some time in the Theosophical Society in Chennai, like one who hesitates on the brinks of a pond on a winter morning before plunging into it. By the time he reached Hardwar, his wallet was empty, but he was unfazed by the predicament. He decided to rough it out. He could have written home for money. He did not; it wasn't pride that held him back from that act—he didn't want them to know his whereabouts, the consequence of which would be being taken back home, willy nilly. Besides, by this time, he had developed a strange, unshakeable faith in the beneficent powers of the cosmos to provide him the bare essentials of life if he was destined to live. (As it turned out, his faith or confidence wasn't misplaced.)

The life of the mendicant began. By no stretch of imagination could that life be called one of ease. He went through trying times, save for short spells of comparative luxury in the form of a wooden cot in a *choultry* and a few adequate meals. But nothing could douse the fire of his determination—he would see his journey to its end.

He traversed most of the region on foot: Rishikesh, Uttarakashi, Gangotri, Yamunotri, Kedar via Buda Kedar, Badrinath and back to Rishikesh. Whenever opportunity provided him, he stayed at various ashrams, for shorter or longer periods. He put these respites from his peregrinations to good use; studying, meditating, learning. He met many interesting *sadhus* and *sannyasins* of different denominations, among them some remarkable men of great spiritual accomplishments. From his first-hand experience, he concluded that the Himalayan environment was highly conducive to meditation and *sadhana*. He was thrilled at the sight of the sacred rivers. His hope to meet the Master (the only one whom M came to recognise as his true Master) of his childhood experience was, however, not fulfilled during this journey. Reluctantly, he came down to the plains, resolving to undertake the search for his Master on another journey.

Now, what? He was not ready to go home. Not as yet. He was, so to say, at the crossroads. He was free to go anywhere. In the event, he proceeded to Mumbai, without any conscious bias towards that commercial city. In Mumbai, he met Swami Hiranmayananda, the then president of the Ramakrishna Mission at Khar and requested the Swami to initiate him into the Order as a *brahmachari*.

M was accepted as a probationer. While there, he kept his Muslim identity a secret. No, he was not resorting to any subterfuge, for he knew that the Mission had nothing against Muslims or people of any other persuasion joining the Order. He somehow felt that he would be the recipient of favourable discrimination, if he revealed his identity.

The discipline at the Mission helped him greatly; he learned a lot without let or hindrance. He read most of the literature of Sri Ramakrishna and Vivekananda and met some of the stalwarts of the Order like Swami Ranganathananda and Swami Tapasyananda. (Many years after M left the Ramakrishna Order, the same Swami Tapasyananda initiated him into the Ramakrishna *mantra*.)

He was with the Mission for three years. The wanderlust struck him again. This time around, he decided to investigate the working of the Ananda Marga. Earlier he had met its founder, Ananda Murti, a.k.a. Sri P.R. Sarkar. M joined the Ananda Marga Training Centre in Benaras . His stay there was extremely brief—less than a month. (To date, he is averse to talking about that phase of his life, more because of his nature not to sit in judgment about any one or anything than because of any unpalatable experience.)

Without much to do and without making anyone the wiser, M slipped out of the Centre. He took a train to Hardwar and Rishikesh. He felt that he was the prodigal returning home.

At Rishikesh, he decided to stay in the Divine Life Society, founded by the doctor-turned-saint, Swami Sivananda. It is an ideal place for a *sadhak*. It is situated on the banks of the Ganga. Yoga and Vedanta are taught in the *ashram*, the senior swamis are mostly helpful; and when one has time one can wander around and meet *sadhus* and seekers of all sects.

That pilgrim season found M again on the road to Badrinath, sometimes following the common pilgrim routes, at others discovering his own path through forests, staying at roadside *dharmashalas* and *choultries* and many a time in forest hermitages beside a river. After many days he reached Badrinath. He managed to commandeer the shelter of a *choultry* to give the much needed rest to his tired limbs. When he tried to sleep, he found that his single blanket was insufficient to fend off the cold, but he did not seek help. The travails of the previous journey had weathered him. Moreover, who would be bothered with anything when the fire of spirituality had burned away all desires and weaknesses that flesh was heir to? He slept.

He woke up next morning, energised and in the grip of an ecstatic mood that stayed with him during the whole of his stay in the region. He says, "The presence of highly evolved souls is almost palpable in these areas. It was so palpable, I even hoped that I would be meeting some of them."

Though M made light of his physical discomforts, they were miraculously relieved by the arrival of a *brahmachari* he had met in the Divine Life Society. This acquaintance had been an intrepid pilgrim and his many pilgrimages had taught him to be resourceful. Soon, he found for M an independent *kutir*, a couple of blankets—even a wooden plank to sleep on. (Recalling it, M laughs, "Five-star luxury".) Above all, he arranged with the Nepali *dharmashala* to provide M food. Thanks to the same benefactor, M came to know the *rawalji* (the chief priest of Badrinath) as well.

As is any pilgrim centre, so is Badrinath, M reminisces. There were all kinds of people congregating there. Many beggars have made it a place for earning their living. For them the saffron robe is nothing more than an insignia—a licence—to beg. Even some *sadhus*, apparently a cut above the beggars, stole each other's *kamandalus* and blankets. Perhaps, 'M' concludes, such goings on might have the sanction of perverted logic: can anyone in a spiritual democracy be the undisputed possessor of anything?' Genuine *yogis* and *paramahamsas* too existed among such a melange; some were indifferent to whom they consorted with; others deliberately mingled with the throng, perhaps, in utter acceptance of the world as it is.

"How does one come across more such genuine souls?" M asked himself and others. He learned and surmised they lived on the other side of Narayan Parvat beyond Badrinath. He travelled thither. All he had with him were his *kamandalu,* a staff and a blanket. On his previous visit to Badri, he had wandered about a kilometre towards his present destination. But the vast territory beyond that lay unexplored.

He walked along the rough terrain, heaving himself up steep mountains and plodding wearily down, again to climb up. He must have covered some six or seven kilometres, towards the confluence of the Saraswati and the Alaknanda, called Keshav Prayag. Close to this place is a cave, about which one *sannyasin* had told him, is the Vyasa Guha. He found himself unable to proceed beyond the *guha*; a strange force seemed to deaden his feet and transfix him to the spot. First he thought the leaden weight of his legs was due to exertion, but he discovered it was not; for his whole being became suffused with an exhilarating bliss. Enough. This was the signal, he knew. He walked into the cave. Inside, it was cold. Slowly he oriented himself to his surroundings. The neighbouring snowclad peaks shed an incandescent light beyond the cave. A soothing calm descended on him. Spreading the blanket on the floor of the cave, he sat in *padmasana* and went into a deep meditative state.

Time, as far as he was aware, stood still; he did not know how long he sat there in meditation. All he knew when he opened his eyes was that the afternoon—he had arrived round about that time—had segued into dusk and darkness. As he blinked his eyes and gradually became attuned to the darkness, he saw before him someone he vaguely felt he knew, someone who was not a character in the lagan of his memory. In a flash, his memory raced to his childhood when he stood awestruck at the backyard of his house, watching a man walking towards him. The meaning for that epiphany was found now. It was not a recollection of a face long forgotten; it was more than that; it was the recognising of a guru he vaguely knew he would find. He found him now indubitably—with a certitude that did not need any substantiation.

His Master in person was the substantiation.

Time had apparently not wrought any change in him. He looked the same as when M had first seen him—a very fair young man with billowy hair, and almost beardless. He smiled and his smile transported M to a different world. M began to laugh without any reason and almost hysterically, and his eyes filled with tears. Even now M cannot recall that experience without a frisson of exultation.

"No hysterics," said the calm voice of the Master, this time not in Deccani Urdu but in English. He stroked or patted M's shoulders. Brought to normal, M touched his Master's feet.

The Master sat beside him. Long into the night and till dawn they talked, the Master revealing the truth he had attained and the disciple clarifying his doubts. At sunrise, which was too soon for M, the Master blessed him by way of farewell and walked away from the cave. It was, however, not a hasty farewell; the Master promised to monitor M constantly and to appear at selected moments and places in the future. (The chapter "Thus Spake the Master" in this book is a personal account by M of one such meeting.)

'When the seeker is ready, so will be the Master' was no more a mere truism to M now. Weren't all these years of disquiet and indomitable search leading him to this glorious meeting with his one and only Master?

He knew that his life would never be the same again. He was thoroughly overhauled; a lasting change in his consciousness took place. He would have followed his Master willingly. (His was not an abject surrender; if it was, it was a surrender thoroughly approved of by his critical faculties.)

But his Master deflected him from that course. He advised M to go back to the plains, join the throng of humanity; he was to be in the world but not of the world without losing the BLISS that was to be his forever.

A new phase of his life began. He continued to travel, yet it was not the travelling of an aimless wanderer. He strictly adhered to his Master's advice to look at the world from close quarters without being blinded by the brightness of its transient pleasures. He did a stint as a journalist which brought him into contact with many eminent people. (A year was spent in the Andamans in the capacity of a resident editor of a daily.) He wrote political commentaries, short stories, and articles on various topics. And he became a trustee of the Krishnamurti Foundation two years before the latter passed away.

His association with J. Krishnamurti was not accidental; his Master had told him to meet this maverick sage. M had earlier heard Krishnamurti's lectures in Chennai and elsewhere and had also read most of his books. So, when he finally met him at the Foundation headquarters in Chennai, M was not altogether ignorant of the renowned iconoclast. He had a private discussion with him lasting some half an hour, which resulted in his staying at the Foundation with the hearty approval of Krishnamurti himself.

M was strictly adhering to his Master's advice; M's association with Krishnamurti was to be a further learning process. If he had made use of his closeness to Krishnamurti for personal self-aggrandisement, that could be termed as devious. But he did not. Theirs was an association of mutual understanding and love. The trusteeship was thrust on him and he willingly demitted it three years after Krishnamurti's death.

His Master had also told him that Krishnamurti was to be the last of the many teachers whom he was to meet. M did not then understand the implication of the prophecy. Now, he understands. It was at the Foundation that he met his future wife, Sunanda, a Saraswat Brahmin whose family hails from Udipi. He now understood the significance of his Master's words: "Be in the world but not of the world." To be in the world, one has to fulfil the duties of a householder as well. M married Sunanda; token apprehensions of such a marriage were easily overcome. They remain happily married and have a son and a daughter.

After marriage and leaving the Foundation, he and his wife ran a free school for the poor and backward people of Rayalpad, a small village in Karnataka. Under the Foundation's aegis, the school ran for over nine years. By then, he was being sought by many for guidance in their spiritual journey and he began to find it an onerous task to manage the school and, at the same time, attend to the needs of his friends. If there was a choice, the decision to choose put him in a quandary. Not for long. His Master, as ever, came to his aid—his forte in this world was decided. (He gave up the school, but not without making arrangement for handing it over to a new management.)

Ever since, he has remained a beacon light to many who have been tossing about in spiritual darkness. Today, he is a highly welcome speaker at many fora in India and abroad, though he prefers to have smaller groups of people to share his wisdom with. And with this in view, and eagerly encouraged by his friends, he has set up the Satsang Foundation, the aim of which is to act as a meeting point for spiritual seekers of all persuasions. This may be the primary aim or function, but M has underscored an equally important function for the Foundation; that of extending a helping hand to the less privileged of our society, like the destitute old. For, as he emphasises, unless spirituality is buttressed with *seva*, self-less service to others, it will be self-defeating. Knowing well that ideas do not go beyond the blueprint stage, M on his own initiative (and with money borrowed from banks) has already built a modest old-age home for the poor near his residence in Madanapalle in Chittoor district of Andhra Pradesh. Enthused by his example, the members of the Satsang Foundation are engaged in raising funds for an extensive old-age home.

With all these activities, as a spiritual guide, as a family man, as a social development activist, has he come to the full flowering of his potential, spiritually or otherwise? Those who know him will answer this in the affirmative but not M. It is not modesty alone that makes him underplay the well-earned regard and respect of his numerous friends and acquaintances; for he believes in the infinite potentiality of man. It is this belief that has propelled him to yet another new area, that of art. He is a self-taught artist of more than average accomplishment and his first public exhibition of his paintings and sketches was immensely successful. In a way he gives the lie to Jean Erdman's statement: "The way of the mystic and the way of the artist are related, except that the mystic doesn't have the craft." This mystic, if you can call him that, has the craft—the noble craft of living life to the full.

If this brief sketch falls short of doing complete justice to M—something he is not bothered about—it can be finally added that his life echoes the words of Dante: "The purpose of the whole (work) is to remove those who are living in this life from a state of wretchedness and lead them to the state of blessedness."

Notes and References

1. *The Rig Veda* by Keegi.
2. A Jewish sect of circa 3rd century BC, which still exists in a modified form.
3. Wherever the pronoun 'he' or its other forms are used, it is only due to linguistic convenience of a time-hallowed practice. No gender discrimination is advocated or implied.
4. There are two types of *kumbhaka: sumyaka* and *kavala.* In the former, the breath is suspended after forced exhalation, and in the latter, the respiratory stillness follows normal exhalation.

2

TOWARDS GREATER GLORY AND A HAPPIER LIFE

1. The Opening

Yes, God exists! And if this sounds like rubbish that intellectuals shun and fools (God bless them!) believe in, I say: "Hold on!"

Don't let intellectual arrogance destroy your being. Think carefully, for you are merely prejudiced. The believer in God is as prejudiced as the atheist for both deny or affirm without due enquiry. It would be better if you say: "Let me find out." Isn't that the correct attitude, the right approach?

Has this wonderful complex world come about by accident? Or, is there a Supreme Intelligence behind all these happenings, however difficult, it is for our puny brains to discover its plans and motives?

On the other hand, do you think the world revealed to you through your sense organs is a real, solid, substantial one? Ask the physicist. He'll tell you: "It's all mere vibration; particles or charges in constant motion or just waves of different frequencies in perpetual flux. Your three-dimensional world is largely a concoction of your senses and mind." And you?

You are the consciousness which is the witness of all the drama, watching in amusement as the ego plays its games, dons different masks at different times and ends up identifying itself with the roles it plays. The real you is that ever-blissful, unchanging, blessed consciousness.

Therefore, enter. Enter the door that opens onto the path that seekers have trodden for thousands of years.

Abandon not the infinite ocean of bliss and happiness that knows no end but is at the end of the road. Some call it 'God', some 'Truth', and some 'Nothingness', for it can't be described by words or gestures.

It is more precious than anything your mind can conceive of and O! how fortunate that this priceless pearl is not far away in some inaccessible part of the world or hidden in the dark bowels of the earth. It is nearer to you than your own jugular vein. It is Bliss Supreme which the sages of yore imbibed and which then made them dance in ecstasy. It is your very 'Self'.

Will you, ignoring this great treasure, play with mere trinkets? It is for this blissful being who shines through every heart that man searches everywhere except within. Like the musk-deer that carries fragrant musk under its own tail and searches for the source of the fragrance all over the forest, under thorny shrubs and under dangerous snake holes, human beings search endlessly for happiness mistaking pleasure—the short interval between sorrows—for the real thing.

But the blissful surprise is right here—so simple and clear. No one need shave his head or wear special headgear or ochre robes or run away from all that one holds dear. No Sir! You may live in this world and do your duties, earn your livelihood, look after those that need your help, spread the fragrance of love and service, and yet remember to keep in touch with your true Self, the spark from the great fire, the drop from the great ocean, by meditating regularly, so that, in the spotless clear mirror of your heart, Divinity's reflection glows. From your heart, then, will the serene rays of the spirit proceed and fill other hearts with bliss.

First, the Lord may give you what you want if you ask with all your heart, and then you will discover what you truly need and seek for it and He shall surely grant it.

"Ask and it shall be given thee," said a great Master, "Seek and ye shall find. Knock and it shall be opened unto thee."

Of course, the master tests your patience. Therefore, knock persistently but wait patiently. Then will your heart be filled with supreme bliss and you will work for the good of mankind.

Sorrows and shortcomings, the cares of this world, are there certainly, but who doesn't have them? Now you, the traveller on the path should know that they are lessons for you, and that after each obstacle is overcome, the road becomes smoother and easier. And overcome you will. There is no doubt.

So let nothing stand between you and the overflowing cup of wine that lies so near and yet so far. Drain the cup and declare: "There is but One, the blissful Truth. Nothing else exists."

Step firmly upon the path. Have no fear. Fearlessness is close to 'Truth'.

2. The Path

Is there a way to the bliss divine? Is there only one way or are there many? As many human beings exist in this world, so do exist many ways, for there is no single magic formula or esoteric rite which will transform one instantaneously. Supreme perfection cannot be purchased off the bookshelf nor by bribing the guru or God. All those are tricks you use in everyday life. They don't apply to the Supreme Self. If someone promises salvation all at once, take care; you are about to be hoodwinked. If someone guarantees to lead you to Supreme Bliss in a certain number of days, again be on guard. No human being can ensure it; only God can.

So there are different paths depending on the kind of disciple, the kind of guru, the special circumstances and other external as well as internal factors. One teacher may be well-suited to a certain kind of disciple and ill-suited to another. The genuine teachers know this. Once in a thousand years or so appears a great Master who can lead one through all or any one of the paths. This is indeed a very rare occurrence.

However, there are certain essential factors of a spiritual journey and these apply to all paths.

1) The aspirant is sincere in his search.
2) He has understood (in theory) what he is looking for, or to put it in another way, knows what he is not looking for.
3) He is prepared to listen and learn without prejudice.
4) He is ready to swim against the stream.
5) He is prepared to practise regularly and diligently.
6) He is patient.

By saying that the aspirant is sincere, I mean that he is not pretending, for various reasons, to be a religious man. He is ready to speak the truth and learn the truth. He does not advertise his religious inclination by changing his robes or overestimating his capacity to renounce, run away somewhere, and cut himself off from his environment. Such actions smell of hypocrisy, and in the end, confuse and confound his own self and others too. True, the renunciant is a very highly evolved being but real renunciation is rare and is no joke.

Moreover, one may live in the world and not be stunned by it. Such persons are needed today. May such aspirants increase in number! May noble thoughts come to us from every side!

Now, what is the sincere aspirant looking for? Why is he doing so? Aren't the pleasures of the senses enough for him, surrounded as he is by all the luxuries of the world?

Looking about him in all directions, while still playing his role in the drama of this world, the discriminating aspirant sees how fleeting the enjoyments of the world are. In his mad race towards the fulfilment of his desires, man does not pause to consider how pleasures are followed by pain, and how, whatever one achieves, there is still a feeling of want, the unending hunger and thirst, a covetousness that never ceases until death with its final blow makes null everything that has been held so dear and ends the race with total extinction. And death is not far away. It lives with us. Isn't death our constant companion? How terrible it would be if things don't die but last forever. It is because death destroys the old that it is made possible for the new to be born, and this process goes on and on. In fact, every second (or fraction of a second) the present dies and becomes the past for a new present to be born. So death is very much a part of life. Don't we die every day, every second, as the present moment turns into the past and becomes a dead thing only to be stored in the memory?

Ask the biologist and he'll tell you; millions of cells die every day, every minute, to be replaced by new ones. And yet when death strikes the individual, he is often caught unawares. No one knows when it comes and the human being likes to believe it is far, far away.

Watching, observing all this carefully, he begins to wonder, what am I seeking? I seek joy, and sorrow raises its ugly head. I get hold of what I desire and then comes the fear of losing it, of somebody taking it away, or losing it when I die. I see the beautiful moon, and time, the great snatcher, snatches it away and I am left with an image I keep craving for again.

I build and nature destroys because it has its own building plans. Today's palace is tomorrow's random rubble. Where is the permanency I seek? Where is the real happiness, the supreme joy that I seek?

Asks the master: "You experience joy when coming into contact with the objects of the world. But the joy wells up in your own heart, doesn't it?"

Does the enjoyment take place in the object or in yourself? All joys spring forth from within your being, my dear friend. The reservoir of all joy, the essence of all bliss, is in your own heart, in the core of your own being.

The *rishis*, the mystics, the saints, have all found the way to tap the source of perennial joy within, without resorting to external objects.

This blissful fountain is your real 'Self', your real being. Search for it with your teacher's help. In fact, you are 'it' and when you discover this, you'll get an idea of what the Higher Self, God Almighty, is.

This 'Self' of yours is ever free, ever blissful. It is and was never bound; therefore, there is no question of making it free. It is always free. It manifests itself as the 'I', the consciousness, the 'I' that exists eternally in the waking state, dream state, and deep sleep, the 'witness' of all states of consciousness. This is the real 'you', the blessed, blissful 'Self'. The mind, borrowing the 'I' from it, mistakenly feels bound and attempts to make itself free.

You are eternally free. You are existence-consciousness-bliss, unpolluted by anything that happens in the relative world. You are free. Shake off the illusion that you are bound and rejoice in absolute freedom and absolute bliss.

You don't need to do anything to be free when you are already free. So, relax and sit firmly and reflect on this truth until your mind settles down, the false movement of constant becoming ceases, and your 'Self' shines forth in all its glory, reflecting the majesty of the higher 'Self'—God.

But alas! The mind does not settle down so easily. Therefore, I shall give you a simple technique discovered by the ancient *rishis*. You don't have to escape to the caves to practise it. Practise in your own house, in the midst of your daily life. Practise three times a day or at least once.

Remember! There is no technique to reach the 'Truth', for you are yourself the 'Truth'. Techniques are there to still the mind so that it understands the truth that the mind cannot reach the 'Self' and settles perfectly, so that the 'Self'—the ever-blissful 'Self'—alone shines forth.

Now, begin to practise immediately and be free. Don't wait; for, every second you lose by postponing is a great loss indeed.

3. Abhyasa—The Practice

Find a quiet corner where you may sit calmly without being disturbed for at least ten minutes every day, preferably twice, at dawn and dusk, or at least once a day. Ensure that there is enough ventilation to allow fresh, sweet breeze to enter. Having chosen the place, don't change it oft.

This has its own advantages. The conducive vibrations of the place in which you practise build up as days go by until they are able to influence your mind the moment you sit down.

This is why many meditators prefer to use a small special room or shrine exclusively for the purpose of meditation. That is, of course, the best thing to do, but if you find it difficult to set apart a meditation room, you could use any quiet corner as I have mentioned above. Even your bed will do, but take care. Since a bed is meant for sleeping, the subtle influence of sleep may overpower you as soon as your mind begins to calm down and you may find yourself falling asleep. This has been the experience of many meditators except the most advanced who can even meditate in the marketplace.

It is also advisable to have a set of clean, loose-fitting and comfortable clothes which are to be used only for meditation.

Although the above are ideal, you do not have to worry too much about the details as long as you can sit down in a quiet place, indoors or outdoors, undisturbed, and practise your meditation.

Wash your arms and face and feet before you sit in a comfortable posture on your seat. Face any direction you like but try to stick to the same direction every day.

First of all, thank the Lord for the food and shelter you have been provided with. Then, if your window overlooks a river or a lake or a forest or a lovely garden, take a good look and observe the beauty of nature. Take a few deep breaths as if you are filling your lungs with the splendour and vitality of nature.

Then, broadcast your love to all of creation mentally and give special attention to those who are supposed to be your enemies. Think that you are filling your being with love with each inhalation and sharing it with others when you exhale.

Now, if you like, before you begin the actual practice, you may perform the usual prayers, rituals, etc., which have been taught to you before. Hindus can practise *sandhya vandana*, or simply chant the wonderful *Gayatri Mantra* a few times. Muslims may practise their *Namaz*, an excellent spiritual exercise. Christians can chant their prayers which include the 'Sermon on the Mount': "Our Father who art in heaven...", Buddhists may chant "The Jewel in the Lotus", the Sikhs their *Satnam,* and so on.

After this is over, sit in a comfortable, relaxed and yet firm posture. *Sukhasana* or sitting cross-legged as one does while eating is fine, or if one has had enough training, *Padmasana* or lotus posture in which Buddha is usually depicted is ideal. Sitting on the heels with head bent and chin pressing the upper part of the chest in a chin-lock (*bandha*) as Muslims sit for prayer—the Egyptian posture—is also suitable. The main idea is to keep the backbone erect and yet not suffer pain or discomfort.

Those who cannot sit in any of these postures may sit on a cushion or chair. It is foolish to try to twist yourself into difficult postures all of a sudden. When there is pain, the mind will remain occupied with it and will refuse to ascend to higher things. So be comfortable but not so comfortable as to fall asleep.

Inhale deeply and consciously a few times. Relax! for, concentration and meditation come with relaxation, not with tension. Then begin to chant any of the well-known *mantras* you might have learnt. *Om Namashivaya* is good, so is *Om Sri Ram Jai Ram* or *Hare Krishna* or *Allah-hu* or merely *hu* or *Om*. The idea is that it should be concise, not long and unwieldy. If you so desire, I shall give you one *mantra*: *'So Hum'* which means 'That I am'.

Now, the important thing is to combine your breathing with the chanting of the *mantra*. Don't chant audibly; chant mentally. When you inhale, chant '*So*', and when you exhale, chant *'Hum'*. Chant nine rounds, one inhalation and one exhalation making one round.

Then—this is most important—give up trying to control your breathing consciously. Instead, allow the inhalations and exhalations to follow their own rhythm. You merely watch the inhalation and exhalation quietly, meanwhile continuing to chant "*So Hum*' mentally with each natural inhalation and exhalation.

Now, fix your mental gaze at a spot just below your physical heart or at the point between the eyebrows. Pinch once lightly any one of these spots you have chosen to help you fix your attention there. Visualise a silvery flame, cool and radiant like the moon, shining in your centre of attention. Or, you may visualise a lovely rose, a lotus, or a star. But stick to any one symbol and centre. Don't keep changing and shifting. Personally, I would suggest a blooming, radiant lotus in the heart-centre but leave it to you to decide.

As you watch your breath silently chanting *'So Hum'*, you will find that the rhythm of breathing slows down considerably and a certain peace and tranquillity begins to emerge and envelope your whole being. Often, at this stage you feel like giving a deep sigh. The sigh denotes that your psyche is beginning to relax and settle down.

The great *rishis* discovered this secret of *pranayama* when they found that a calm, slow rhythm of breathing always accompanied a tranquil mind and a fast breathing pattern indicated tension and agitation. You can discover this for yourself if you observe your breathing and mind under various circumstances. This is true *pranayama*, not the forced holding of breath which could cause internal haemorrhage or worse.

As you calmly observe your breathing, and as the breathing pattern becomes so slow and soft that you can hardly feel it, stop even watching the breathing, and fix your attention only on the lotus that blooms in your heart. Abandon even the '*So Hum*'. Just sit there, feeling the blissful presence of the Lord, who is bliss itself, filling your heart with the nectar of joy. You are yourself that joy.

As you practise daily (and with the master's help which is surely there) you'll enter subtler spheres of consciousness and bliss. You will see lights and hear heavenly music and witness wonders, but tarry not. These are merely signposts and sometimes temptations. Keep marching ahead quietly until you come face to face with the 'Presence', who is within and not far away.

At times, your breathing may even cease briefly. This is *keval kumbhak* but there is a greater *keval kumbhak* where there is cessation of all thoughts. There is no incoming thought or outgoing thought. There is only the 'One Pure Witness', unaffected *Satchidananda*, watching the drama.

Of course, in the beginning, thoughts will come, sometimes in torrents, but don't worry. Don't try to throw them out. Watch calmly as you would a mischievous child and they'll settle down and disappear.

Thoughts are like ripples that disturb the calm surface of the mind and distort the reflections. When they disappear, the surface becomes clean, and the undisturbed reflection of the 'Sacred One' is glimpsed, however briefly.

What is important is to understand that you are really the ever free, radiant, blissful being, and sit quietly. Everything else is rubbish and cannot harm you in any way. "Meditate and discover this," said the *rishis* of yore.

When you get up from your daily meditations, thank everything and everybody with utter humility.

4. Benefits

What benefits does one derive from the practice of the technique discussed above?

You will soon begin to experience a lightness of body and mind. You will be less tense, less agitated, and in the business of daily life, more efficient. Modern medicine has discovered that many physical ailments have their beginning in mental stress. You'll be saved from them on account of the relaxed condition of mind that you are able to induce daily. Since a tension-free mind can think more clearly and without confusion, you'll see that your thought processes begin to get into top form.

True, the dirt and rubbish that you have gathered in the past will at times come to the surface, but don't worry. That's how they are thrown out and got rid of.

You'll also begin to get a new feeling of unselfish love and compassion towards other living things. From the lower centres, the thrill will ascend to the heart centre above, and whenever you encounter a beautiful thing, be it a bright flower or a lovely peak, or an old solitary tree, your heart will thrill with divine bliss.

But all these things are, so to say, fringe benefits. The real goal is still not attained. Don't also mistake the technique for the goal. Go on meditating deeper and deeper until the mind is stripped bare and you find your own dear 'Self', the radiant unpolluted, indestructible, pure consciousness, the unalloyed bliss. May the master guide you in this supreme adventure.

5. Adjuncts

Is it enough if one just meditates twice a day or five times a day?

Not exactly. From times immemorial the sages and prophets have laid down what are called rules of conduct which a religious person should practise. While rituals and ceremonies may be dispensed with if found unnecessary and cumbersome, the rules of conduct have to be studied carefully and adopted as far as possible, because, by practising them, your capacity to meditate is enhanced.

Given below are the *yamas*, the do's, and the *niyamas*, the dont's, common to all aspirants no matter what formal religion they belong to:

Do not steal.
Do not kill.
Do not lie.
Do not be violent.
Do not commit adultery.
Do not indulge in intoxicants.
Eat in moderation—do not overeat.
Pray or meditate daily, if possible, twice a day.
Treat your parents and teachers with respect.
Lead a simple life.
Do some service to other human beings.

You'll notice that all these precepts, if practised, are surely conducive to peace and tranquillity. If you steal, you always have the fear that you will be caught some time or the other. How can such a mind be calm and meditative?

If you kill, you know that it is most likely that you will be killed by someone too. The whole culture of violence where enemies kill each other is merely the symptom of a disease which lies deep in each individual. The desire to kill is necessary to win the race, but then who pauses to ponder over the fact that all joy and fulfilment lie within the heart and not outside? The same blissful Self which is in you is in me and one has only to meditate and live in peace to contact It.

If you lie once, you'll probably have to lie again and again to protect the original lie, and so on it goes—a vicious circle. Soon you have spun a web of lies which you are afraid might be broken and further lies are woven to prevent this. Soon, you even begin to believe your own lies.

How can such persons have peace of mind? So, throw all these things overboard and lead a simple, transparent life full of peace and tranquillity. The small inconveniences you may feel are nothing compared to what you gain.

Now adultery. Spiritual progress is linked to the ascension of the mind into subtler and higher states of consciousness, the grossest points of which function as hunger and sex. These are perfectly legitimate needs of any human being. However, we pay too much attention to the latter, because it affords the maximum enjoyment we can normally conceive of, and for a split second, even makes us forget ourselves.

As one approaches subtler spheres, the consciousness has to be shifted from the lower centre of sexual satisfaction to higher centres of spiritual satisfaction. This cannot be done if one's mind is always centred on sex-related activities. Therefore, the emphasis on moderation in sexual indulgence. The ideal person does not go around indulging in sex at all times under all circumstances and become a prey to venereal disease or

AIDS or other physical and mental diseases, all in the name of freedom. He gradually gets rid of the obsession by sublimating his sexual energies to higher emotions which lift his consciousness to greater and higher states of existence. In the upper centres, like the heart centre, for instance. He enjoys a bliss that is a thousand times more powerful than mere sexual enjoyment. Therefore, the advanced *yogi* needs no sexual enjoyment in the usual sense of the term.

Closely connected to sex is the question of food. The best way to control a wayward mind is an occasional fast. The *yogi*, a practitioner of spiritual exercises, needs to moderate all his activities in order to be able to progress in his endeavour. Mark you, moderation is the key word.

The *Gita* puts it succinctly: "This yoga is not for him who eats too much or too little, who sleeps too much or too little." That sums it up. While it is true that vegetarian food is indeed conducive to meditation, especially in the beginning, it is also true that vegetarian food can be made so rich and spicy as to cause lethargy—a sure obstacle to meditative states. There are also people who overeat and claim it is all right as long as it is vegetarian food. Surely, overeating is a *tamasic* act, not a *sattvic* one.

Don't be obsessed with what you eat and what you don't — a trait which Swami Vivekananda called 'the religion of the kitchen'. Eat what is nutritious, what your body needs. Take medical advice if necessary but eat in moderation. If you see somebody eating food which you do not fancy, do not imagine that he is an ignorant person or a spiritually undeveloped one. Remember that Swami Vivekananda ate meat and the great saint Ramakrishna loved fish. Of course, this does not mean that you should eat fish or meat because they did. Use your common sense.

Vegetarianism by itself divorced from other factors may not be the sign of a saint. Hitler was a pure vegetarian. He did not even eat eggs, but was he a saint? How many thousands of Jews did he send to the gas chambers?

As far as intoxicants are concerned, one doesn't have to be extraordinarily intelligent to understand why one is advised to abstain from them. Anything that makes one unbalanced and lose one's sense of proportion and judgement has to be abandoned.

Your reason is a very important instrument and an intoxicant destroys it gradually, apart from causing physical ailments and the curse of alcoholism or other forms of addiction. The habitual drinker or drug abuser overestimates his abilities and commits blunders. Many road accidents are the result of drunken driving. The false sense of euphoria and self-importance induced by alcohol or drugs is followed by depression. Ask the addict how he dreads his hangovers or cold turkeys and yet he waits eagerly for his next high. Addiction is slavery, mental and physical, be it alcohol or drugs. Drugs are, however, the more dangerous of the two since they can cause permanent damage to the brain.

"Okay," some may say, "are we to cut out all that we enjoy from our lives? If we don't drink occasionally how are we going to get away from the sorrows and cares of the world? We will become more frustrated, more violent. There is no other state of altered consciousness that we know of."

Now, wait a minute. You are not cutting out every joyful thing from your life. You are only exchanging lesser joys for the springs of joy that can well up within your heart. You will no longer complain when they begin to flow.

Have a better substitute, a better addiction right away—the wondrous wine of chanting the name of God, singing for Him, in Him, about Him, pouring out your love to Him, playing musical instruments, dancing before

Him: O! how sweet are the lovelorn songs of Meera, how heavenly the strains of her *tambura*. Sing and dance to your heart's content. Absorb yourself in devotional music and let it carry you to higher states of consciousness. Once you taste the wine of devotion, you'll never want to touch lesser intoxicants.

But let me caution you. Music must be pure. Full of devotion. It shouldn't degenerate into cheap entertainment. Also, it is only a means to an end. Don't forget that the aim is union with the Divine Lover, or as some others might put it 'sieving the ore to discover pure gold'.

Now the question of service. No one can meditate or remain engaged in devotional activities for twenty-four hours a day. There may be exceptions but we are talking of the general run of mankind. Therefore, find some time when you are engaged neither in earning your bread nor in praying to do whatever you can for your fellow human beings.

The only gods you can actually see with your physical eyes are these living gods. Serve them but remember while doing so to be thankful to them for providing you the opportunity to serve them and thereby speeding up your spiritual progress. It is you who should be thankful, not they. Feed one hungry man even once and see how much easier it is to contact the Divinity when you sit down for meditation that day.

Someone asked me the other day, "Sir, are we to begin meditation after we have practised all these moral precepts to perfection?"

That, Sir, is next to impossible. No one has ever succeeded in becoming morally perfect before beginning to meditate. The fact is that meditation and practice of moral precepts complement each other. Begin to meditate today. Do not postpone it. Side by side with this, attempt to follow the *yamas* and *niyamas* to the best of your ability.

As you progress, you'll become more and more morally perfect and so also will your progress in meditation become better and better. This will go on until you reach your final goal. Till then, there are bound to be imperfections. So don't worry. Only when one has perfectly understood that all that exists is the 'Self', will selfishness be completely destroyed. Doesn't all immorality spring from selfishness? As you approach nearer and nearer the blissful Self, you will find no need to behave immorally. Until then, do your best. Conquer hate with love.

6. The Lover

While all these instructions apply to most people, there is one exception—the true *bhakta*, the lover. He or she is caught up in a cyclonic love affair as it were with the Lord, the eternal sweetheart, and no rules and regulations apply to such fortunate souls.

Meditation, diet, religious observances, customs and manners, duties and responsibilities, none of these matter to this being. He throws the whole world to the winds and pines away for the Lord. Separation from his Beloved is unbearable for him and he goes mad with longing. He is unaware of anything else. And when the Lord finally comes, he doesn't bow down to Him. They, the lover and the Beloved, are then locked in the embrace of divine love until they cannot be distinguished, one from the other.

But a word of caution. Do not try to imitate him. Also, guard yourself against imitations. The one sure sign of a true lover is the absence of selfishness. If anyone pretends to be one and you discover even a tinge of selfishness, keep away.

True lovers of God are rare and, wherever they are, a flood of spirituality sweeps through and many are benefited by it. And yet most of such lovers refuse to be masters or guides since they are most of the time caught up in their own world of divine love.

A few of them, after having passed through the stormy stage and attained the highest, bring their minds down to everyday consciousness in response to the Supreme Being's command so as to teach others. Such teachers are indeed the greatest and fortunate indeed are their disciples.

But, once more I must warn you. Some mentally unbalanced persons and lunatics may behave like *bhaktas*. So take care. Absence of wisdom and presence of selfishness and lust are sure signs of fake *bhaktas* and lunatics.

The *rishi*, the *jnana yogi*, and the *raja yogi* are of a different type. They are calm, collected and tranquil, and can often teach even without uttering a single word. Silently they guide and transmit the energy which cleanses your heart and clears the passage for the ascension of Divine Power which is the very essence of bliss.

7. The Master

When the time is ripe, the master comes. You don't have to search for him in the Himalayas. He may be living next door but you may not know. Your ignorance and arrogance effectively help him to remain hidden.

If you are a sincere aspirant, if your only goal in life is to meet your beloved 'Self', if you constantly meditate and pray for guidance, the master shall surely come—if so required.

You may or may not recognise him but he guides you silently. The true master is the Lord Himself who takes on various forms to guide the devotee.

Test the master well before you accept him. If there is even a trace of lust or selfishness in him, he is not of the highest status. Test him thoroughly but have patience.

Do not judge in haste, for, many a time the actions of a master have been misunderstood. Mysterious are his ways. Do not judge his actions without finding out the motives.

Once you have decided after careful reflection, treat him with the greatest respect and beg of him to accept you as a disciple. You are fortunate if he does, because a true master is not fond of collecting hundreds of disciples. Rarely does he agree to be the guru.

A guide is necessary in almost all cases because you are starting on a voyage of largely uncharted territory. You may find here and there greatly advanced spiritual beings who do not seem to have had a guide. They are exceptions, and though they may not have a guide in human form, understand that God Himself guides them and looks after their needs.

Don't imitate them, for they belong to a special category. Do not even imitate your own teacher for you are not he. Follow his teachings and instructions instead and you'll bloom into a master in your own original way and not turn out to be a faint imitation; a shadow of the original.

A master may be young, old, male, female, fair or dark. The externals do not matter at all. What matters is his inner spiritual status. He may, if he so decides, help you wipe your heart clear of all the accumulated *vasanas* and make you free.

May such a master guide you!

3

THUS SPAKE THE MASTER

Though M came across many saints and sages who helped him in their own way during his years of extensive wanderings as a spiritual seeker, he never regarded any of them, albeit his respect for them, as his guru. He knew he would have no guru other than the Master (as M calls him) whom he had seen, as it were in a vision in his childhood, and who had promised to be M's spiritual mentor. However, M did not deliberately seek him out, confident that his Master would meet him at the appropriate time. In the event, not only did he meet him many times, but once, on their third encounter, they spent a fortnight together in a cave at Kedarnath. This stay turned out to be a watershed in M's life; the course his life took on from then changed and led him where he is now.

The following chapter is a recollected transcript of the dialogue between the Master and M. The latter asserts that many of his doubts were cleared by these sessions of questions and answers stretching over the length of his stay. To reproduce it in the same format is warranted by a noble tradition—a tradition by which most religious literature of the world (the *Bhagavad Gita* to name but one) is handed down in the form of catechisms, *prashnottara*. An advantage of this method is that, as a form of communication, it is far superior to a discourse. In this method, the teacher answers questions from an earnest student rather than haranguing a medley of captive students with different degrees of interest in the subject. Hopefully the spirit of the dialogue informs this reproduction.

An interesting aspect of this conversation is that it was not recorded mechanically or manually at the time of its occurrence. It was not due to M's lapse or lack of eagerness, especially as he was sceptical about his, as he thought, too fallible a memory. His Master dissuaded him from such an attempt; he said that this was unnecessary. He assured M of a total recall at the right time, though what that 'right time' was left unclear.

A few years later, M was working as a journalist in the Andamans. Often afternoon time lay heavily on his hands and he decided to test his ability for total recall. He won—rather, his Master did not fail him. To his amazement and delight, the entire dialogue began to unspool, and words flowed as if he were engaged in automatic writing on the papers in front of him. It is hoped that the result—a permanent record of the dialectical exchange—will clear some of the doubts of the readers as it did that of M himself.

It was a chill Himalayan night. We sat facing each other on a large flat boulder in front of the cave. Around us, the silvery, snowclad ranges glowed in celestial light. In spite of the crackling fire we had earlier set ablaze and the thick blankets wrapped around me, I was shivering when the icy wind blew across my face. My guru presented an utter contrast to my swaddled and cocooned form; he sat there bare-bodied save for the single knee-length cotton loin-cloth tied around his waist. He had, I learnt later, mastered the yogic technique of adjusting his body temperature by the practice of what the Tibetan *yogis* call *tumo*. He appeared very comfortable on the folded woollen blanket. Sitting in *padmasana* (lotus posture), he looked at me with a kind and beatific smile.

"Relax," he said. "There's nothing to fear. Be comfortable." I don't know what happened then. His words acted as magic on me; my tired body, hauled all the way up the almost inaccessible peak, was miraculously revived. My aching muscles no longer ached; my blistered feet tortured me no more; even the wind seemed to stop its needle-pricks. A soothing warmth flowed from him to me and permeated my whole body. I suddenly found that I was not hungry anymore, though I hadn't eaten for three days and had been ravenous till then. I was once again steady of body and mind; I became alert with an acuteness I never knew I had possessed before.

This was the first day of the fortnight I spent with him. I had so many questions to ask and so many doubts to clear. I didn't know when again I would get such an opportunity.

And we began.

M: Sir, I have studied Vedanta for many years. When I began, I thought I understood everything, but as years passed and I went deeper into the subject, I began to realise how little I had grasped. There are so many questions that have remained unclear.

First, unravel the mystery of knowledge itself, since this very path of the seeker is known as the path of knowledge, *jnana marga*. I am as confused as many by the statement made in the *Isha Upanishad*:

Andham tamah pravisanti ye vidyam upasate
tato bhuya iva te tamo ya u vidyayam ratah.

(They who worship ignorance enter into darkness
And they who worship knowledge enter into greater darkness.)

The first part is clear. We have always been taught from childhood that ignorance is to be overcome by acquiring knowledge. So, it is quite baffling to hear the *rishi* say that, to worship knowledge is to enter into greater darkness. How can this be? If both ignorance and knowledge lead to darkness, is there something beyond both knowledge and ignorance? If even knowledge leads to darkness, what is it that one can reach which is beyond both knowledge and ignorance?

Master: Now, be alert son. To be alert is not to strain but to relax and let the teachings sink deep so that you'll have no more doubts. Listen carefully, and after that, ask me further questions if you have any. We'll discuss matters as two close friends discuss their intimate problems. Let's have complete frankness and love between us.

Yes, many have been perplexed by the apparently contradictory statements of the *Upanishads*. But, if you examine them carefully, there are no contradictions.

"They who worship ignorance enter into darkness." Isn't that quite clear? Ignorance, *avidya*, is lack of knowledge, nescience. It is by acquiring knowledge, *jnana*, that ignorance is destroyed. Nowhere does the *Upanishad* say: "Don't acquire knowledge", for knowledge is the only instrument that can dispel ignorance. Everything that we learn is knowledge, including what you are hearing from me now. Then, how can knowledge lead to darkness?

Listen carefully. The *Upanishad* doesn't say that knowledge leads to darkness. All it says is that those who 'worship knowledge' enter into greater darkness. This is to be examined closely.

Let us say that you have walked into a field full of thistles and you have quite a few thorns lodged in the feet. You did not know—you were ignorant—that it was a thorny terrain. You try to pull them out with your bare hands, but to no avail; they are in too deep for that. So, you find a sharper, longer, sturdier thorn to remove them. Similarly, you remove the thorns of ignorance and pain with the thorn of knowledge. Tell me, will you, after getting rid of the painful thorns, stick the larger thorn into your feet? No, you won't; you will throw it away. So is it with the thorn of knowledge used for removing the thorn of ignorance. Both of them are discarded by the *yogi*, the seeker, whose aim is liberation.

Before we go further, let us see what knowledge itself is. You understand a thing or an event and say, "I've acquired knowledge of that." This means that you have stored all the information or as much as you can get regarding that thing or event in your memory, so that you can refer back to it, recognise and react to it, in the future. All knowledge is like that—that which is stored in one's memory. Can you think of any other? The moment you have listened to my words, they have vanished from the present and have become things of the past. They constitute memory, and memory is a thing of the past. Knowledge, as we know it is then something that you remember, whether it is from the recent past, a split second ago, or years ago. That is, it is memory. All knowledge is, therefore, memory—a thing of the past.

On the other hand, *Brahman*, the Ultimate Reality, is never a memory, never a thing of the past. It is the living present, the eternal, immediate present and, therefore, can never be comprehended by knowledge, which has only the past as reference.

M: If knowledge refers only to memory, what is it that can know *Brahman*?

Master: To understand it even conceptually, we may have to go into different kinds of knowledge. At the lowest end is *ajnana*, knowledge about the world obtained through our sense organs. Higher than *ajnana* is *jnana* or knowledge of the Self and other things acquired through the reasoning intellect, *buddhi*, and from scriptures and teachers. Still higher is *vijnana*, discriminative knowledge, that is able to differentiate the real from the apparent or relative.

One who has reached the level of *vijnana* can hone it to perfection by trying to remain constantly on that level.

If this is done, the intellectual understanding of *jnana* and the passion-arousing *ajnana* and even the earlier stage of the discriminative capability, *vijnana*, are overcome or transcended, thereby attaining the intuitive and unitive experience of *Brahman*.

In this context, even the word 'experience' is a misnomer, a wrong term, because it implies an experience and, therefore, an object of experience. All that can be said about such a state is that it is a mental/ spiritual enlightenment where nothing but an all-pervasive knowledge exists without the duality of the knower and the known.

M: Am I then to understand that knowledge, as we generally understand the term, is useless?

Master: No, certainly not. The capacity for knowledge, whatever its level of perfection, is the highest faculty of man. Each level in the hierarchy of knowledge I talked about has its proper place. Without experience derived through our senses, however unreliable or unreal they may be, we cannot apprehend our immediate world of living. They may lead to passions, attachments, and so on, to cause misery or fleeting pleasure. Yet, it is the same misery or pleasure that often moves one towards *jnana* or reasoning intellect to assess and evaluate the condition we are in. Reason, then, leads to *vijnana* through an intellectual appreciation of a higher Reality. However, reason itself can show that reason is often unreliable, coloured as it is by our subjective prejudices. When reason is aided by intuition from a source unknown and unknowable, one reaches the level of *vijnana*, and the Ultimate Reality becomes no more an intellectual concept but a potentially and presently experiential one.

Constantly remaining in that state, one attains *Brahman*, the Ultimate Reality. In other words, *Brahman* is beyond *ajnana*, *jnana* and the early stages of *vijnana* and is realised in deep meditation when the mind, which is nothing more than a collection of thoughts, is transcended. Knowledge, which is memory, a thing of the past, comprehends fully how finite it is, and therefore, how it cannot reach out to the infinite from which intelligence itself proceeds. Giving up all reasoning, arguments and doubts, it then lets go of the chain of thoughts and becomes as still and placid as an infinite expanse of clear water without a single ripple in it.

It is in that calm, mirror-like, pure mind that the ultimate, absolute, blissful Reality[1], the *Brahman* is reflected.

This is what the *Kenopanishad* means when it says: "That which even the mind cannot reach but because of which the mind acquires the faculty to comprehend; That, O seeker! is the true *Brahman*, nothing that you worship here."

M: But, doesn't the mind become inert like that of an idiot by ceasing to think and reason?

Master: How can the mind which reflects the very seed and source of intelligence ever become inert? Such a mind is ever active, ever engaged in doing what has been ordained as its duty. Such a mind, blessed by an abundant rush of energy, as it is linked to the very fountainhead of the tremendous energy that operates the entire universe, is not ruffled by obstacles or failures. It gets neither dejected by failure nor overjoyed by success. It is a mind that works steadily without the distractions that the ordinary person has. It is only such a mind that can be truly said to function, charged as it is with the energy from the Universal Generator. The rest are all inert because they have not discovered the secret of work.

The only experience or state of being whose content cannot be subrated (subrate—a mental process whereby one disvalues some previously appraised object or content of consciousness because of its being contradicted by a new experience) in fact and in principle by any other experience—which no other experience can conceivably contradict—is the experience of pure Spiritual Identity; the experience wherein the separation of self and non-self, of ego and world, is transcended.

Let us look at the minds of some great persons who were not merely thinkers but doers. Adi Shankara[2] was one of the foremost exponents of *Advaita Vedanta*—I shall go into it later—and he was a *sannyasin* par excellence. In a short span of 32 years, he did what ordinary people would take a hundred years or more to accomplish, or perhaps, would not even accomplish in quite a few lifetimes. He travelled on foot through the length and breadth of this vast country, wrote voluminous commentaries on the scriptural texts, engaged numerous scholars of the day in debates, and renovated temples wherever he went. And he was successful in everything, for he had understood the secret of work.

Take a more recent example, the great Vedantist, Swami Vivekananda. One cannot but be overawed by the stupendous work that the Swamiji did. What a towering personality and what a tireless worker for the good of humanity! You yourself can think of many examples.

M: Sir, what about those who prefer to remain silent after realising the Ultimate Truth?

Master: If the perfected sage prefers to remain silent—no doubt there are scores of pretenders to that perfection—that silence is more effective than speech or overt action. The sage works silently on the minds of those who listen to the Voice of Silence. Such a sage has reached the source of all thought and can change the entire world by a single thought. That silence is more potent than hours of lectures. Silently—as silently as the lowly grass on which we tread—such a sage works miracles, while himself remaining hidden, like the ultimate *Brahman* Itself. By a single thought of such a sage, Herculean tasks are executed.

Now, I'll explain another aspect of the statement, "They who worship knowledge enter into greater darkness."

Some people, when they have studied the scriptures and the numerous commentaries and other branches of Vedic knowledge like astrology, mathematics, *mantras*, and so on, get puffed up with pride and begin to strut about, pretending to be learned men. Their ego is so bloated that they begin to think that they are always right and refuse to listen to or deign to consider the point of view of others. Their mindset cannot accept that there may be some other way of looking at the same problem or view which they might have failed to grasp. Their hubris—their excessive pride—is invariably the cause of their downfall and their consequent misery. Such people's minds are closed by prejudices and preconceptions and are like stagnant pools. Their minds lose their sensitivity and alertness and are tarnished and beclouded by dross that they mistake for knowledge, since it has been acquired painstakingly over a long period. Theirs are the jaundiced minds that see yellow everywhere and in everything. They are the worshippers of knowledge who enter into greater darkness; they refuse to turn to the light and keep denying its existence. Some of our scientists and philosophers can be included in the ranks of these worshippers of darkness.

I shall illustrate what I said by a story. There was a great God-realised saint to whom seekers used to flock to learn the Truth. A puffed-up scholar too went to him for instruction. After listening to the saint for a short while, the scholar asked, "How soon can I achieve the liberated state, Sir?" "After a long time," said the teacher.

A poor illiterate gardener, who was also there at that time and was listening to the saint with rapt attention, got up and thanked the saint with folded hands, saying, "Sir, I don't know how to thank you for what you have taught. I am an ignorant man. Will I ever attain the highest?" "In a few days," said the teacher.

This answer piqued the scholar. "How is it," he asked, "that this ignoramus can attain the highest in a few days while I, a great scholar, shall have to wait for so long?"

Unruffled by the scholar's hubris, the saint said, "Your mind is so cluttered up with things that you have collected that it will take a long time for you to unlearn all the misconceptions you have already formed. Your ego is so swollen up that it has shut the door of understanding and simplicity through which Truth enters. The moment you are free of all this rubbish, you will attain the highest. It is to remove all this dirt that I have given you so much time."

M: Does this mean that the ignorant have more chance to know the Reality than the learned?

Master: Certainly not. I was giving you an illustration to show that memorising dozens of scriptures cannot make one learned. A truly learned person is one who has the capacity to grasp and understand and not merely memorise. It is only a mind that is free of misconceptions that can understand—because of its intellectual sharpness—that, however high the intellect may soar, it has certain limitations, a certain dimension beyond which it cannot reach; for, it cannot reach that fourth dimension wherein resides the very source from which arises the unique human capacity of thinking, the mother of all thoughts.

M: I don't understand very clearly what you mean by the fourth dimension.

Master: Many people don't. It is difficult for a person who is accustomed to a three-dimensional world of length, breadth, and depth (height)—whose thoughts are conditioned by these limiting dimensions—to conceive of a fourth dimension beyond the mind itself. It can be experienced only when the entire chain of thoughts—the very thought process—is totally quiet and silent. Only by living in it can it be understood. But I'll try to explain it as logically as possible. At least, you'll be able to grasp it intellectually, and contemplating upon it, perhaps, experience it.

Imagine two wafer-thin, red-coloured, disc-like creatures living in a large box without a roof. They move on the floor of the box in all directions. They obviously cannot move outside the box because of the restricting walls of the box. Inside the box, they are capable of moving in all directions but have no capacity to move up or down the walls. They can move only along the length and breadth of the box. Having been born and brought up in the space in which they live, they have no conception of any dimension other than the ones they are familiar with. Height and depth don't exist for them and they have never been able to venture out of their square space.

Let us say, someone dips his hands into the box from atop and lifts one of them and transfers it to a similar box in which live creatures that differ only in being green in colour. In the same way, a green one is transferred to the other box.

Both the green and red creatures are at a loss as to how such a transference occurred. They cannot conceive of a movement upwards and downwards, since they are used only to lateral movements. For them, any movement other than the horizontal is a miracle and they continue to live in their new environment, aware of only their two-dimensional space.

Most of us are like these imagined creatures. We cannot conceive of a dimension other than, or higher than, the world of our normal sense organs—sight, hearing, touch, smell and taste—and the limited world of the intellect which itself is conditioned by the world of sensory experiences. The spiritual journey begins only when the alert intellect recognises the possibility of another dimension where it cannot—constituted as it is—reach by normal means of thought or sensory perception, and starts exploring other means to reach there. It is even hard to believe that there are a few who have come upon this lofty dimension, for the conditioned mind finds it difficult even to visualise it.

An adaption[3] of the parable of the Greek philosopher, Plato, states the same thing in a slightly different way. In a long underground tunnel, just wide enough and high enough for a person to stand, moves a line of slaves connected to each other with iron chains running from their shackled legs. Their hands are also manacled and their heads restrained from movement by heavy weights hung from their necks. They have been there from the time they can remember. They can move only in one direction—forward. They can see only in one direction—front. For years, they have been walking inside the circular tunnel endlessly. The only rest and relaxation they can avail themselves of are the rare intervals when they are allowed to lean on the walls of the tunnel for a while before resuming their ceaseless, monotonous movement.

On the roof of the tunnel, there is a door which opens into the world outside. Of what use is it to them who cannot observe it, each one of whom can only view the back of the one in front by the faint light seeping from the door above?

It happens that, by accident, the manacle, the shackle, and the weight that restrained movement snap and fall off from one of the men. Used as he is to his mechanical mode of movement, he doesn't become aware of this and continues to follow the rest until, one day, a sharp pain in his neck forces him to turn around. Immediately, he realises that he can do what the others cannot—move his head in directions other than he is used to. He also finds that he can lift his legs and move with more freedom.

With his new-found freedom of movement, he looks up and sees the dim light coming in from the opening. Though he continues to walk in the procession, he has a growing hope that he might be able to operate beyond the limitations of the others.

One day, someone comes to the opening and calls him. At first, he pays no attention. But, when the man above becomes insistent, the slave stretches out his hand to be lifted up out of the tunnel. At first, the bright glare of the light dazzles him and he is almost blinded. Guided by his rescuer, he gets accustomed to the light gradually and understands what a wide, free, and beautiful world exists outside. He also realises that he can move and act as he likes.

He is the man who has reached a dimension of perception that is beyond the circumscribed view of those inside the cave. What would be the reaction of his cave-mates if he visited them later and related to them the wonders of a completely different world of freedom and light? They would not be able to grasp the fact that what he is telling them is the truth. They would be sceptical and call him a liar or a mad man, until they themselves become free to reach the new world, the new dimension, that he has reached.

The man who got free is the wise sage and his doubting friends, who continue to move like automatons, are men chained in a cycle of life and death, living in ignorance.

There you have the teaching in a nutshell.

* * *

[It was past midnight by then. My Master bade me sleep on the plank inside the cave, while he himself continued to sit in *padmasana*, steady and erect—a majestic bare-bodied figure who, like Arjuna, seemed to be a *gudakesa*, conqueror of sleep. I, on the contrary, went into a deep, relaxing sleep and woke up in the morning, completely refreshed.]

* * *

M: As you cleared my doubt on the statement on knowledge in the *Isshvasya Upanishad*, so would I like to understand the essence of the *Shanti Mantra* of the same *Upanishad*:

Purnamadaha, purnamidam /
Purnat purnamudacyate /
Purnasya purnamadaya /
Purnameva avasisyate.

That is complete, this is complete;
From that completeness comes this completeness.
When completeness is taken away from completeness,
Completeness alone remains.

It is rather confusing and I often wonder whether it is a play on words.

Master: No Vedic statément is a mere play upon words or something said for the fun of it. The *shanti mantra* you quoted just now is nothing but the law of conservation of energy as it is now known to scientists. As you know, the law of conservation of energy states that energy or its equivalent in mass can neither be created nor destroyed. It means that the sum total of mass and energy remains constant. Nothing extra can be added to it nor can anything be subtracted from it. That completeness is *Brahman*—the ever-complete Reality that exists even in the so-called vacuum.

Just as this completeness which is matter or the world of the senses can be transformed into another form, energy, but which can neither be created nor destroyed, so does *Brahman* manifest in various forms and cannot be subjected to addition or subtraction.

Incidentally, in ancient numerology, this quality of indestructibility was represented by the mystical figure 9, because when the digits of any multiple of 9 are added together the result is again 9.

M: Sir, please explain now the Vedantic teaching: 'The world is unreal'. How can the world which is so palpable, which we can see, touch, and feel all the time be unreal?

Master: It is certainly a major, perhaps, the most important, question. We'll have to look at it from various angles, one by one.

Let us first take the question of seeing. We see the sun rise and set every day with our own eyes. Does the sun really rise or set? Science tells us that it doesn't; that the sun remains stationary and that it is the earth that revolves round it. Of course, the scientists have adduced proofs to support their observation. Against this present unassailable truth, our sense of sight tells us that the sun rises and sets regularly. Are we to believe our eyes or the evidence of scientific data? Isn't the information collected by our sense organs, then, often false?

M: Yes, I agree. We can't believe everything that we can see. Sense perception can be an illusion.

Master: We'll analyse now why Vedanta declares the world to be unreal.

Everything that exists in this world is constantly in motion. Night gives way to day, life to death, and then to new life again. Millions of cells of your body die every minute and new ones take their place. What is here today is not there tomorrow. Can anyone catch the present as time speeds on? The moment a thought is born, it has vanished into the past. No ordinary man knows where it all began or where it is going to end, if it ends at all. Can something which appears and vanishes like a bubble, something that is not permanent, be ever real?

Reality is permanent, eternal. Nothing that keeps changing and is temporary can be real. The only unchanging, undecaying reality is *Brahman*.

Let us examine the question of the reality of the world of the senses more closely. For the purposes of analysis, let us consider a small wooden cube painted green. The first characteristic that distinguishes it from other objects is its colour. The light spectrum, the rays emitted by the sun, consists of violet, indigo, blue, green, yellow, orange, and red, the colours you learnt to remember by the acronym VIBGYOR. During our schooldays we have also seen the experiment in which a disc painted with these colours, when rotated fast, showed only a white surface as a proof by analogy of the resolution of light. We have also seen a second experiment in which a beam of white light is allowed to refract through a glass prism; it immediately resolves into the seven colours of the spectrum.

Colour, then, is a property of light. When we say that an object is green, that is not strictly true. What we see as the green colour of the object is due to the cube absorbing all colours of the spectrum except green, which colour it reflects. Any object that absorbs all the colours and reflects none appears as black, while one that reflects all the colours looks white.

So, the only quality that any material has by virtue of its molecular structure and chemical composition is that of reflecting certain colours and absorbing certain others. Paints of various colours are manufactured by the technologist who knows that, if a particular chemical, say A, is mixed with a certain other chemical, B, the resulting product will have the quality of reflecting, for instance, the green colour. With the same chemicals, process, and proportions, he cannot create another colour.

What concerns us, therefore, is the basic question: 'Is the colour green a quality or attribute of the wooden block before us?' In fact, the green may look like an entirely different colour in artificial light.

M: Yes, I agree that the green colour of the cube is not its intrinsic quality or attribute.

Master: So, the first attribute, the so-called colour of the object is not really its attribute at all. Colour, therefore, cannot be the attribute of any object; it is the quality of light that falls on the object or, if we are colour blind, what our limited colour perception presents to us. Isn't then, colour an illusion?

Let us now consider the shape of the object of our example—a cube. It is an object, as we understand, contained by six equal squares. When we look at it, we do not see all its sides at the same time. By observing any three sides of it at a time, we decide that it is a cube. What happens is that the rays of light that reflect from the object pass through the lens of the eye and form the image of the object on the retina behind the lens; not the entire image, but one, two or three sides of the object depending on the angle of vision and the size of the object. In spite of this partial data, our brain concludes it to be a cube, unconsciously seeing the other sides beyond our vision. Of course, the entire process takes place in a split second and we call it seeing.

You might also have noticed a contrary phenomenon. If you look out of the windscreen of a car awash with rain, you will see the straight electric posts bent and trees and other objects having shapes different from the normal ones. Yet another instance. If you look through a glass plate with an irregular surface, the human face will appear distorted in grotesque caricatures.

Now, imagine a creature born with eyes of different structure from those of human beings. For all you know, this creature may see as a curve what appears to us as a straight line. It might see as a globe what we see as a cube. You wouldn't believe it if it talked to you about its version of shapes.

M: But this uncertainty is only with regard to seeing. How about my sense of touch, Sir? I should be able to feel the shape of the cube.

Master: As we cannot see all the sides of the cube at the[4] same time, so are we unable to feel all its sides at once. In this instance, we conclude that it is a cube by mental juggling of the partially realised tactile impression and visual perception. You know the famous story of the six blind mendicants and the elephant and how each came to his own conclusion as to the shape of the animal. You can conduct a practical experiment about your sense of touch. Take two glasses, one with luke-warm water and the other with cold water. Dip the index finger of each hand, one in the luke warm water and the other in the cold water. Take the fingers out and immediately plunge them in the two glasses in the reverse order. You will find that the finger plunged from the cold water into the luke-warm water feels that it is much hotter than the finger lifted from it had felt it to be.

Thus, we see that two of the attributes we thought as intrinsic of the cube are not really their characteristics. That is, neither colour nor shape is indubitably the attribute of our example; the cube has, therefore, lost its colour and shape on closer examination.

The third attribute that we shall take up now is the size. Size is again a relative concept. Our cube is, let us say, four inches long, four inches broad, and four inches high according to the standards of measurements that we have fixed. The size as seen by the naked eye is purely relative. If you look at it from afar, it might appear smaller than when seen from near. Or, imagine a tiny creature like an ant facing the cube; it would see it as a block of formidable proportions, more like a hill which it would have to climb or go around to reach the other side. If the standard of measurement it follows is the same as ours, it is still a four-inch cube. However, for the ant, the four inches will be more like four miles. For us, a grain of sugar is very small but, to the ant which carries it, it might be of enormous weight. Yet again, a child sees its father as a tall giant but not so when it grows up. So, you realise that size too is relative and depends upon the observer.

Now, where is the cube with its commonly acknowledged attributes? What is its real size? Is it big, small, or tiny? There can't be any definite answer to this question.

M: But, what about mass, Sir? It is a solid; I can feel it.

Master: We'll discuss the solidity or the massiveness of the cube first. Presently, we'll go into your capability to feel it. Imagine a microscopic, virus-like organism that enters your body. It is so tiny that the pores of your skin are large gates through which it enters with ease. For it, our bloodstream might be flowing rivers in which it can swim about and our arteries and veins may be huge tunnels. Your solid body is not solid for the virus which, being smaller than a single cell of your body, can even enter into your bone marrow.

Let us look at solidity from another angle. As you know, all so-called solid matter consists primarily of atoms bound together, so to say, by empty space. You, of course, cannot see this empty space with your naked eye. But the magnified image under the microscope shows the solid matter for what it is—non-solid empty space.

Let us go a little further. What is this minute atom itself? A central nucleus around which the electrons revolve like the planets in the solar system. The nucleus and the electrons occupy very little space in the total area of the atom.

Now, one might ask, "How about the nucleus? Isn't that at least solid?" Again, you find that the protons, which along with the neutrons constitute the nucleus, can further be split into mesons and other sub-atomic particles.

So, where is the thing that you call solid mass? Our *rishis*, who have gone deep into these subjects by virtue of their special faculties, have found that matter is ultimately simply a field in which different forces act and react.

With one more example we shall dismiss the notion of solidity. A piece of cloth is impenetrable to the pressure of your finger; you can't push your finger through it unless the cloth is very old or you tear it. That is, it acts as a solid. But, under a magnifying glass, you'll see the same piece of cloth as having many spaces between its warps and woofs. A microscopic creature can easily pass through these. To that creature, it is not solid and impenetrable but vast spaces with no obstructions at all. Isn't, then, mass too relative?

By closely examining all that is generally considered real, we realise that it is only apparent or relative. Except for the cosmic forces, there is nothing that can be called real. You'll apprehend this reality only by the higher experience.

Finally, there is one more characteristic of our example—its weight. The concept of weight can be demolished fairly easily. Weight is nothing but the gravitational force exerted by the earth. That explains why things start floating the moment they are away from gravitational pull or attraction. You would have seen pictures of cosmonauts floating in their spaceships that have reached beyond the earth's gravitational field. That is, weight also is only relative.

Now, we'll take up what you call 'feeling'. You may say that you feel that something is hot, cold, soft, rough and so on and so forth. By that, what you mean is that you make use of one of your sense organs like tongue, finger, etc. How reliable are they? For example, if you walk into a darkened auditorium from a bright outside, you won't be able to see anything inside. On the other hand, if you walk in with one eye closed and then open it inside, you'll be able to see the inside of the auditorium with that eye, while the eye that has been kept open cannot see it. That is, you feel darkness around you with one eye and experience visibility with the other. Provided that both your eyes have normal vision, which one is being true to the immediate environment and your feeling? Similarly, immediately after eating liquorice, if you eat sugar, it won't taste as sweet as it should generally taste. Where is the sweetness of sugar gone? Where is your ability to taste the sweetness gone?

One can go on multiplying such examples indefinitely. Isn't it sufficiently clear by now that, what we take for granted as the reality of objects or the infallibility of our sensory perceptions, is an illusion, a construct of our mind, our thoughts, and our feelings?

That is not to deny the existence of objects or our ability to apprehend them. What is to be understood is that the world is real only in a relative way but it cannot be real in the absolute sense. Yet, the relative reality is essential only as far as it concerns our functioning in the world; no more no less. Unfortunately, to accept it as the absolute reality is the error we fall into and therein lies all our misery.

Since you have a scientific bent of mind, I shall compare the need to accept the relative reality of the world with that of accepting Newtonian laws to explain many phenomena in the visible world or even at the atomic level. However, when we come to the sub-atomic world, the same laws are found inadequate, if not entirely useless.

The modern mind is very much inclined to dismiss what our ancient sages and saints stated about the insubstantiality of the world. But today's science is inclined to accept it. Otherwise, why should a physicist say a few years ago: "Our conception of substance is only vivid so long as we do not face it. It begins to fade when we analyse it .... The solid substance of things is another illusion .... We have chased the solid substance from the atom to the electron; there we have lost it."

It is this uncertainty about the actual nature of the objective world that is termed as the great illusion. Only the mere existence of it can be acknowledged; not the form in which it appears to exist.

The absolute reality behind these illusions might appear abstract, but it is abstract only in the sense that it is beyond the reach of our senses conditioned to the practical, yet illusory, needs of our day-to-day world. According to our scriptures and sages, this abstractness called *Brahman* is the only true reality, the only true existence. Our intellect can go a step further than our senses only to understand that *Brahman* cannot be intellectually grasped. That pure existence, *Brahman*, ever existent behind the constantly changing forms or the insubstantiality of the world, is realised only in deep meditation, beyond the intellect and the mind, when thoughts have utterly ceased.

"That", the *rishis* proclaim, "art thou", after they have understood it. Actually, there isn't even 'thou'; only 'That' exists.

* * *

(A method of attaining 'That'—the Absolute Reality or *Brahman*—is most effectively enunciated in the *Mandukya Upanishad* belonging to the *Atharva Veda*. Though considered the shortest of all the 108 known *Upanishads* having only twelve verses, *Mandukya* guides the seeker to Reality by systematically showing him how to reach the Divine within. Since this *Upanishad* points a way to the necessary intellectual background for developing a higher life by rigid analysis of the different states of consciousness, it appeals even to those who are sceptical about religion as conventionally viewed. The following is an exposition of it by my Master—M.)

M: Sir, I have had the opportunity of studying the *Mandukya Upanishad* and I know that Gaudapada's *karika*, gloss, on it is exhaustive. But I have been unable to fully grasp the import of the statements, especially on the different states of consciousness.

Master: I shall again start with a story as a first step to explanation.

King Janaka, who came to be known as *Raja Rishi*, sage among kings, once had a dream. He dreamt that he was a beggar walking around with his begging bowl, hungry, tired, and in tattered clothes. On waking up, he found himself amidst the splendours of the palace.

This set him thinking, "Am I a beggar or a king?" While in dream, he felt clearly that he was a beggar. The pangs of hunger and weariness were no less real than the luxuries of the palace when he woke up. As he was unable to solve this puzzle, he sought the aid of his preceptor, the great sage, Yajnavalkya, who explained to him the different states of consciousness that make this world real, unreal, or non-existent. Though this story has no direct link with *Mandukya Upanishad*, the topic discussed is the same in both, except that the *Mandukya* treats the different states of consciousness as its main thesis.

Now listen carefully. The different states of consciousness are *jagratavastha*, waking state, *swapnavastha*, dream state, *suptavastha* or *sushupti*, deep dreamless sleep, and *Turiyavastha*, transcendental state that lies beyond the earlier three. Consciousness functions in all the three earlier states. When one is awake, the dream state seems to be unreal but, during dream, no reality other than the dream reality exists. And this is so real that all the senses function, all the emotions are experienced. In dream, people laugh, weep, fight, have sex; in short, the dream world is a real world in itself.

But the difference is that the waking state lasts longer than the dream state and, therefore, it is relatively more important and real. Also, in the dream state, there is no awareness of the difference between the two states. In deep dreamless sleep, neither state is perceived by the consciousness, as if consciousness itself were non-existent.

In the dream state, the subtle sense organs of the subtle body which function in that state, replicate the actions of the five sense organs of the waking state like seeing, hearing, etc. In deep sleep, not only these organs, both physical (gross) and subtle, but also the mind, cease to function. *Ahamkara*, loosely translated as ego, individuality, or I-factor, ceases its extrovert activities and traces its way back to the finer part of itself called *buddhi*, the intellect, which is the basic consciousness in a human being that feels "I exist". Since the *ahamkara* does not function during deep sleep, the feeling "I exist" is not experienced.

In deep sleep, all the experiences of the waking and dream states seem to have disappeared and the consciousness enjoys peace and bliss without being impacted or affected by the external world of senses or the internal world of dreams. The paradox of this state is that, on analysing the experience, one cannot know whether one was conscious or unconscious. All that can be said is that it is contentless or negative consciousness, or a consciousness not aware of itself. You may, however, ask whether there is any consciousness during deep sleep which can enjoy peace and bliss. How could there be absence of consciousness if, on waking up, one feels and says, "I had a wonderful, undisturbed sleep"? Undoubtedly, there has been something while in deep sleep which is capable of experiencing that state of tranquillity and which is able to differentiate it from the experiences of the waking and dream states.[5]

Turiya, the fourth state, is not one of the states like the other three. It is present in all the states; even in that state of pure consciousness when *ahamkara*, the I-factor, is dropped. It is this consciousness that is called the *Atman* or Spirit and is the sole witness of waking, dream, and sleep states as also of the various altered states of consciousness like trance, *samadhi,* etc., however lofty they may be.

In *Turiya,* consciousness is in its pristine purity and has no separate identity from that of the all-pervading Universal Consciousness, *Brahman.*

Hence says the *rishi*, "*Ayam Atma Brahma*, my *Atman* is *Brahman*." It is the attainment of the same Consciousness which is referred to by the statement *Aham Brahmasmi*, I am *Brahman*. No one can proclaim "*Aham Brahmasmi*" and remain a limited human being for, where there is even an iota of *aham*, the I-factor, there cannot be Absolute *Brahman*.

The point to be stressed again is that *Turiya* is not comparable to the waking, dream, and deep sleep states. In all these three states, there is a sense of self-identity; there is a subject and an object or an experience and the experienced, even though such a distinction is unmanifest or realised at the time of experiencing. In *Turiya* there is no distinction between the experience and the experienced or the subject and the object, and it is that consciousness that is subject to disturbances and changes. In the other three states, the relative consciousness specific to that state excludes the other states. For example, in the dream state, the reality of the waking world is absent and vice-versa; the king becomes a beggar and the beggar becomes a king. On attaining *Turiya*, the experiencing individual selves are subsumed under the Universal Self or *Atman*. He who has attained or merged in *Turiya* can see the *Atman* in all three states when he descends to relative consciousness. And, for the *Atman* which never ceases to exist, all the three states are mere illusions like different moving pictures seen on the same screen.

That person is the true *Sannyasin* or renunciant who is untouched by anything whatsoever, who is ever established in the bliss of *Brahman*, irrespective of his activity or inactivity. It is only he who is fully relaxed and at peace, for he is even beyond deep sleep and rests in the calmness of that which is the root of all activity. He is the sole witness to the rising and falling of the waves of creation and destruction.

* * *

For one who is established in *Turiya*, therefore, the entire world of experience is like a long dream from which he has woken up. He is face to face with the Ultimate Reality beyond all dreams; in fact, he himself is the Reality.

* * *

My *guru* began, "Today, we'll discuss the question of the *yogic* eye and some more about the mind and how the same mind that binds and conditions you can also open the channel through which flows abundant energy from the cosmic motor.

I'll again start with a story. Stories are the most suitable as explanatory illustrations; even small children understand them.

One day, a wisened old man in rags was literally dragging himself along the side of a busy road in a big city. He was so emaciated and weak that every step he took seemed to be a painful ordeal. All of a sudden, a car coming at full speed screeched to a halt, its horn blaring, just behind him. Now, almost a miracle took place. The old man who, seconds ago looked as if he would fall and die any moment, leapt on to the footpath at a safe distance and far from the car.

How did he do that? A moment earlier, he couldn't have had any inkling of the imminent danger, so that he could save himself. Then, what saved him? It was a split-second reflex action. The message 'Jump and save your life' must have flashed into his brain from the Supreme Director, and the message was transmitted instantly to his limbs. Adrenalin was released immediately and the muscles reacted.

The point to note here is that there was no interference from the conditioned mind and the prejudiced thought process. If thought had interfered, he couldn't have jumped away from the wheels. He would, instead, still be having thoughts like, "How can an old, weak man like me jump out of the car's way when I don't even have the energy to walk?" while the vehicle crushed him under its wheels.

In this emergency situation, the message 'Jump' came directly without being conditioned and influenced by thought; he was directly drawing energy from the cosmic motor, although involuntarily.

What this man achieved involuntarily is achieved by the *yogi* voluntarily. The *yogi* learns the technique of quelling the otherwise constant vibrations or ripples of his mind and making himself receptive to the flow of energy from the Cosmic Mind whenever he feels the need. This is the secret of the first sentence in that masterpiece of *yoga*, *The Patanjali Yoga Sutras* which says: '*Yoga chitta vritti nirodha*'; that is, yoga is the elimination of the *vrittis*, the disturbing waves of the *chitta*, the mind-stuff. This is how the *yogi* gains access to the cosmic source of wisdom and energy. Not only does he develop the capacity to receive messages but also to send messages, as it were, to the fourth dimension, and to get answers.

The main centre he makes use of for this purpose is the brain, which is the seat of the mind, and more specifically, the two major centres of the brain known in *yogic* terms as the *ajna* and *sahasrara chakras*. Note that the word used is *chakra*, meaning wheel. Actually, *chakra* implies a whirlpool-like area, a junction where the cosmic energy can be observed by a clairvoyant, whirling constantly and exhibiting myriad colours. It is through these centres that the cosmic energy enters the human body.

Yogic anatomy identifies each of these (major) existing *chakras* with a corresponding nerve plexus on the spinal chord of the human system called the *sushumna nadi*, the central channel. The exceptions are the upper two *chakras* which are intimately connected with the functioning of the two tiny ductless glands, the pituitary and the pineal glands situated in the brain.

Starting from the lowest, the *chakras* are the *muladhara* at the base of the spine, the *swadhisthana* slightly above it, the *manipura* at the level of the navel, the *anahata* at the level of the heart, the *visuddha* in the area of the neck, and the *ajna* and *sahasrara* I mentioned earlier.

* * *

I shall explain now the secret of *Laya Yoga* or *Kundalini Yoga*.

In every human being resides the negative aspect of the cosmic energy called the *Kundalini Shakti*, coiled three and a half times and symbolised by a serpent, at the base of the spine in the *muladhara chakra*. But in all, except the *yogi* who has mastered the technique of awakening this energy, it remains inactive, although potent like a coiled spring. Using the technique—which can only be learned directly from a *guru* and not by any other means—the *yogi* succeeds, by constant effort, in awakening it and leading it upwards, piercing *chakra* after *chakra*, to finally reach the *sahasrara chakra* at the top.

As the *kundalini* pierces each *chakra*, the conduits are cleared of all impurities that have been blocking them and the communication channel with the Cosmic Being is opened up. As the *kundalini* ascends and each *chakra* is opened up, the *yogi* reaches newer and newer dimensions of power; his links with the Cosmic Energy become close, and he attains the capacity to work wonders.

The powers which he exhibits are called *siddhis* in *yogic* parlance. The perfect *siddha* is the one whose *kundalini* has opened the *sahasrara chakra* and who, thereby, has attained the capacity to harness the very source of Cosmic Energy.[6]

Now, I'll tell you more about the *ajna* and *sahasrara chakras*. These are the most important ones that have a direct bearing on knowledge. The *ajna chakra* is situated in the forehead, just behind the point where the eyebrows meet. It is also known as *trikuta* or *bhrumadhya* and is symbolised by the third eye of Shiva, who is himself the symbol of transformation and regeneration. It is when this centre is activated that the practising *yogi* becomes clairvoyant. He acquires the ability to use the *chakra* as an instrument to perceive subtle forces in dimensions beyond the world of sense-perception.

Just as a drop seen under a microscope reveals it as a complex, ever-active system of dancing particles, the universe reveals its mysteries to the *yogi* who uses his special perceptive faculty of the *ajna chakra*. He thus comes to possess knowledge that the ordinary man does not have access to. The *ajna chakra* is also the transmitting station from which the *yogi* can send messages in the form of thought-waves to other humans or to highly evolved beings who inhabit other subtle spheres.

The *sahasrara chakra* is the highest centre and is the receiving station for all messages from all highly evolved spiritual beings who run the cosmic show. Therefore, when the *kundalini* reaches this centre and activates it, the *yogi* is able to link directly with the Lord of the Universe; he will then be in a trance state called *samadhi*.

This accounts for the immense wisdom that great *yogis*, who are even considered illiterate, display when they have attained *samadhi*. The pineal body, now considered as a vestigeal organ without any known function, has a major part to play in activating the *ajna* and *sahasrara chakras*. I shall teach you later how to harness these energies. The main point to remember is that the practice of *kundalini yoga* is intimately linked with the sublimation of sexual energies, but not by repression, suppression, or any forcible method.

M: In the practical exercises you taught me relating to the *kundalini* yoga, there is a lot of visualisation; one has to imagine so many things. What bothers me is the thought that by allowing my imagination to grow, wouldn't I be cut off from reality and live in a perpetual dream world? Is imagination a sign of mental progress or decadence? Please enlighten me.

Master: Thought is the mother of all action. So also is imagination or visualisation the key to all achievement.

Imagination is not the sign of a diseased mind. On the contrary, it is the sign of a healthy and rich mind. Only when it is not controlled or is allowed to run riot, does it become harmful. Controlled and deliberate imagination is, in fact, the sign of a genius. Great scientists, artists, indeed, men in all fields of endeavour, have always had a rich imagination. The very beginning of any creative venture is imagination.

The artist, for instance, visualises everything in detail before he puts it on canvas. Ask a successful and wealthy man and he will tell you how he, in his days of poverty, had visualised in great detail the house he would live in, the car he would drive, the clothes he would wear, the money he would handle, once he came by his riches. By keeping these images constantly in his mind and working hard on the ideas that flashed out of his subconscious to feed these images, he has his dreams translated into reality. That is regarding the world of senses.

In the subtle world, the result is instantaneous—one doesn't have to wait for long. Every passing thought leaves its impression on the invisible world of fine matter that surrounds us. But, when a particular image is deliberately contemplated upon, and that too in full detail—colour, form, shape, and so on—a strong image is actually created in the subtle world, often referred to as the astral world. When this image is sufficiently strong, it can be used to influence even entities on this gross earth. Great *yogis* create good thought forms and direct them towards those humans who are in need of them. Black magicians use evil thought forms to frighten, and in some cases even to kill, their victims. Only the *yogi* who has reached the highest level is able, by a mere thought, to transform his vision into physical reality. Such persons are rare and should not be confused with *tantrics* who transfer objects from one place to another without any visible means of transport, or magicians who merely perform sleight-of-hand tricks. However, such rare, divine persons, as a rule, never demonstrate their powers except under certain specific conditions.

So, develop the habit of visualising good and beautiful objects—for instance, a full-grown rose or the letter *'Aum'* in Devanagari script in electric blue or gold—every morning in your mind's eye and spread happiness and goodwill mentally to the whole world as you wake up in the morning.

Visualise your desires in complete detail and you are sure to attain them; but never visualise harm to others, for that will arrest your own spiritual development and put you back a few steps down the ladder of spiritual evolution. You can imagine yourself to a state of happiness or unhappiness; it is your choice.

M: I have my doubts cleared about imagination. But I am puzzled by the *yogic* statement: 'The meditator and the object of meditation become one in deep meditation.' If I contemplate a tree, how can I become one with the tree?

Master: You have misunderstood the meaning of the sentence as so many others have.

There are three stages in meditation. In the first stage, *dharana*, one concentrates on a particular object. When the smooth flow of concentration continues uninterrupted for a long time, one is in *dhyana*. The culmination of *dhyana* is *samadhi*, in which state the meditator forgets himself and the only idea that exists in his mind is that of the object that he meditates upon; then, nothing but the object exists for the time being. In that state, the object is peeled off layer by layer and the *yogi* derives knowledge of the object in all its aspects and ramifications.

Those who follow the path of discrimination, the *jnana yogis*, however, interpret it in a slightly different manner. According to them, 'the experience and the experienced are one'.

To make it clearer, let me ask you a few questions. When you say that you are meditating on, for instance, '*Aum*', what happens?

M: I close my eyes and imagine a golden-coloured '*Aum*' shining in my heart.

Master: Who imagines the '*Aum*'?

M: I; my mind.

Master: When you say, 'I', doesn't that mean the whole collection of thoughts that is your mind, your past experiences, your emotions, your reactions, etc.?

M: Yes, that's true.

Master: Isn't the '*Aum*' that is visualised, which is another form of thought, also part of your mind?

M: Yes.

Master: So, isn't the differentiation between the collection of thoughts you called 'I' and the '*Aum*' that is visualised an artificial partition raised by thought itself? Isn't the experience and the experienced both thought—the mind itself? Then, where is the difference between the experience and the experienced? They are the same entity—the mind—a collection of thoughts.

M: I understand what you mean, Sir. When the artificial barrier disappears, all that remains is the field in which so many thoughts appear and disappear. And, as I watch the appearing and disappearing of thoughts, perfectly aware that I, the watcher, am only a part of that unceasing wave of thoughts, I should become calmer than I was ever before.

(Here, without any conscious attempt, I entered into a meditative state, for how long I don't remember. The incessant thought waves must have lost their identity and merged into the source from which they were created; for, when I came out of that state, I felt an inexpressible and inordinate bliss of silence and peace. My *guru* must have watched me throughout and understood my state, for his next words were, "Bless you. Continue to enjoy that ocean of peace with the full awareness that you too are only part of the field of thoughts called mind and you'll lose your finite identity. What will be left over is the infinite, thoughtless reality—the Supreme Peace.")

* * *

M: Sir, *pranayama* is considered a great aid in meditation. How does it help a *yogi*?

Master: You have touched the crux of an important misconception—by associating *pranayama* only with meditation and *yogic* practices. It is a common error.

Another error is to mistake it for one of the difficult and sometimes dangerous *Hatayogic* practices. I must make it clear that *pranayama* is a true science and, in its proper form, it should be taken up by all for their benefit. It helps them as much as it does the *yogi*.

Before I give you some practical hints—which many students of *yoga* may not have come across—let me tell you that many of the secrets of *pranayama* have applications in material welfare as well. If you wonder how a practice that yields material benefits can be useful for spiritual progress, you should know that *Vedic* teachings are not, as generally supposed, concerned only with spiritual salvation, liberation, or *moksha*. They deal as much with *dharma*, the pursuit of righteousness; *artha*, the acquisition of wealth; and *kama*, desire or pleasure. They deal with the how and why of good conduct whether one is a householder or a *sannyasin*, the business of living that includes trade and commerce or any activity contributing to material welfare, and the legitimate satisfaction of one's desires.

That is why, according to *Vedic* tradition, the entire lifespan of a person is divided into four stages called *ashramas*.

The first stage is *brahmacharyashrama* when a person apprentices himself to one or more teachers to learn all that will equip him for the next stage, *grihasthashrama*. In this stage, he is fully engaged in the life of the world, which means marriage, children, earning a livelihood, etc.

Once the duties of the world are fulfilled and the children are grown up to fend for themselves, he and his wife together seek places of solitude like a forest, *vana*, to contemplate on the mysteries of a higher life, a spiritual life. This is called *vanaprasthashrama*.

The last stage is *sannyashrama*. In this, a person, who has contemplated on the world and the subtle spheres and has more than an intellectual grasp of the insubstantiality of the world decides to renounce it for a life that leads him to the Ultimate Reality, while sustaining his body as a mendicant.

Sannyasa, mind you, is adopted voluntarily; one is not bound by any law or compulsion to this *ashrama*. In fact, there have been great spiritual luminaries who remained householders till the very end of their earthly existence. If a person, by virtue of his great detachment and dispassion, took to *sannyasa* he was, however, given a special place in society and regarded as divine. There have been such great souls even in our recent memory.

Most people have to pass thorough all these stages. It is the rare exceptions who, having worked out all their *karmas*, drop the two intermediate stages and leap straight from *brahmacharya* to *sannyasa*.

The real science of *pranayama* does not mean the forcible control or retention of breath; it means the study of applying the laws under which the *prana* or the life force operates in the human body and affects it physically, mentally, and spiritually. If you bear in mind that *prana* is not just the air that is breathed in and breathed out but the magnetic cosmic energy sustaining the body, then you will realise that its proper utilisation is of great importance, spiritually or temporally. In other words, it is not meant only for those interested in spiritual salvation. Those who are caught up in the day-to-day business of life too can derive material benefits of *pranayama*. Perhaps, after attaining their material well-being and still continuing with the practice, they may gradually enter the field of spiritual endeavour by virtue of the proper control of *prana*.

Bear in mind that *prana* is not the air that is inhaled or exhaled but the bio-electric cosmic energy that enters and leaves the body with each exhalation and inhalation; it can be controlled by one who knows the theory and practical techniques of *pranayama*. The etheric energy, *prana*, interpenetrates solids and gases; it is everywhere.

The body absorbs and radiates this energy. According to the *yogic* science, since it is bio-electric in nature and is in circulation, the human body acts as a magnet consisting of two poles similar to those in a magnetised iron bar. Vertically, the head and the upper half of the body correspond to the earth's north pole; the lower half and feet, the south pole. The right side of the body is regarded as the north pole, and the left as the south pole. Similarly, the front and back of a person are considered north and south poles respectively. That is why the position in which one functions or rests is very important.

For example, when we go to sleep, keeping our head north pointing and feet south pointing ensures a tension-free, restful sleep. In this position, the direction of the body is in accordance with the direction of the earth, thereby maintaining a harmonious balance with the earth's magnetic field. If you sleep in the east-west direction, it creates a disruptive magnetic field and affects even your health and longevity. However, when it comes to work or executing any movement as part of your work, it is better to perform it in the east-west direction. All work executed in a north-south direction will be ineffective.

I shall now tell you about the channels through which the bio-electric energy flows. According to *yogic* science, especially *Sivasamhita*, the entire nervous system is a delicately interwoven network of 72,000 nerves or *nadis*. Of these, only three are considered important channels of energy from a practical *yogic* point of view. They are the *sushumna*, the *ida*, and the *pingala*.

The *sushumna* is the organ through which the energy is conducted. The *ida* and the *pingala* coordinate and control all the voluntary and involuntary functions of the human body which an adept can manipulate at will. The *sushumna*, which is linked to the spinal chord, is the central channel, and the *ida* and the *pingala* are situated on either side of it. The *ida*, which is on the left of the *sushumna*, starts from the left nostril, and the *pingala* on the right of the *sushumna* from the right nostril. Both terminate at the coccyx or *muladhara*.

Here is an important secret to remember. The breath does not flow through both the nostrils at all times in any human being. The flow of breath alternates between the two nostrils every 90 minutes. The *yogis* have understood the importance of the shifting cycles in influencing the various states of the mind. I shall just give you a hint on how this occurs.

You must have heard of the functions of the two hemispheres of the brain about which modern neurosciences have given their findings. So, you may be aware that the right hemisphere, which controls the left side of the body, influences visual imagination, music appreciation, intuitive perception, etc. The left hemisphere, which controls the right side of the body, is the seat of such capabilities as language acquisition, logical and analytical thought, sense of rhythm, etc. By constant practice of *pranayama*, a *yogi* becomes an adept at activating at will either of the hemispheres. You too may gain this ability through your practice.

* * *

M: With all the knowledge that I have acquired from you, do you think that I will succeed in my path if I have not much faith in you? I ask this question purely out of academic interest. Please enlighten me about the proper place of faith in religious pursuits.

Master: Faith is nothing to laugh at. The entire world, including that of science, depends a great deal on faith.

At school, you study all about the universe in your science books. Since you are not in a position to explore what has been stated—for instance, that there are nine planets in our solar system that revolve round the sun—you accept it on faith. Of course, as you grow up, you might get an opportunity to find out for yourself whether what you have accepted on faith is true or not. But till then, you pin your faith on the sincerity of the scientist who stated it and the textbook that you read.

Would it not be foolish to deny the existence of the nine planets straightaway because you haven't seen or you can't see them? Of course, the really intelligent student wouldn't either accept or deny it straightaway; he would accept it on faith till he finds a means to enquire into it first hand.

This is the kind of faith that is required of the earnest religious seeker. He has to merely suspend judgment about the truths the sages have uttered after experiencing what is beyond the ordinary man's capacity to explore. In the meanwhile, he should try to develop in himself the faculties that lie outside our sensory organs and conditioned thought. Once he has reached the same state as a sage who proclaimed a particular truth, he is at liberty to accept or discard it. One who denies a statement without enquiry builds a mental obstruction that blocks all knowledge. How can one seek something which one has denied off-hand?

Vedanta, therefore, encourages healthy discussion, and many of the *Upanishads* are in the form of discussions between and among various *rishis*, teachers, and their disciples. These discussions are serious because they are sincere joint efforts to arrive at the solution to a specific problem and not mere indulgence in futile sophistry, parading one's knowledge or the pastime of an idle hour. They are the very essence of Vedantic study and serve to sharpen the intellect of the seeker to help him deal with subjects of a subtle nature.

You should also note that the word translated into English as 'faith' is, in the original Sanskrit, *shraddha*. Faith is not an accurate translation of *shraddha*. Indeed, there are many words in Sanskrit that do not have a one-to-one equivalence in English. *Shraddha*, apart from meaning faith and confidence in oneself, also means one-pointed attention, the sacred care given to one's endeavour. When a person has unquestioned faith in his own capacity for achieving his goal, whether spiritual or temporal, he is not disturbed by negative thoughts that weaken the will and discourage the spirit. Not disturbed by any demoralising thought, the person who has faith in himself persists in his efforts till the very end and attains what he sets out to do.

That is why it is said that faith can move mountains. That kind of faith does not contradict reason but complements it. Have faith in your essential divinity, son, and you'll achieve what looks impossible. Test your faith certainly by trying to gather first-hand information and experience but these moods of doubts and scepticism will gradually vanish. A person becomes totally doubtless only after he has attained *Turiya*.

* * *

(By this time, nearly a fortnight was over. Given the option, I would have remained with my guru till my mortal life came to an end. That was not to be. To make the best use of the little time left of my stay, I persisted in learning more and more from him. His answer to my importunity was the following.)

Master: There is a limit to everything including the dose of teaching that can be given at a time. Too much would go to waste since your mind would not be able to grasp it; too little would give you the idea that that is all there is to knowledge and, therefore, you are all-knowing. Your eagerness to learn more shows that you realise your shortcomings. And it is a good sign; the sign of a sincere student.

Anyway, before you leave, I'll tell you a story that will be of great use to all sincere seekers.

The story is of Ananda, the great disciple of Buddha. In spite of his devotion to his master, he once became extremely agitated and perplexed by what seemed to him an unsolvable problem. Doubts assailed him so much that, apart from the scriptural question he was trying to solve, he came to question the very teachings of his teacher. Conflicting emotions overwhelmed him and, as an escape from his anguish and restlessness, he began to pace the rough ground with such an intensity that his feet began to bleed. Yet, the solution to the problem remained elusive.

The Buddha had been watching him for some time. Moved by the turmoil of his beloved disciple, the Buddha beckoned to him. "Ananda," he said, looking kindly at him, "bring your veena and play me a lovely tune. Relax now. We'll tackle your problem later."

Ananda was a highly accomplished musician. He brought out his veena and was on the verge of playing, when his master interrupted. "Slacken the strings," he said. Ananda was perplexed at this strange command but he obeyed. "Now play," the Buddha said. "How can I when the strings are slack?" said Ananda. "All right," said the Buddha, "tighten the strings." When they became taut enough to play and he was ready, the Buddha said, "Tighten them more." "The strings are sure to snap, my Lord," said Ananda.

The great teacher smiled. "Ananda, I have no need to listen to music. Whenever I have the need, I can listen to the music of the spheres. I took you through these motions only to bring home a point. Just as the strings of a veena should be tightened only to an optimum limit for tuneful music, so should the mind be stretched to its right limit for effective performance, no more, no less. A lazy mind, like the slackened strings that produce only dull noises, can have only hazy and sluggish thoughts. Similarly, a mind stretched beyond its capacity is tensed and incapable of clear thinking. In such a mind, thoughts rush in so fast that there cannot be coherence. Leave alone coherence, such a mind is likely to collapse under the strain and that can even lead to insanity. The key to clear thinking and problem solving is, therefore, an alert but relaxed mind. Concentration is not tension. On the contrary, it is possible only when the mind is relaxed but attentive."

Ananda got the message.

M: In the case of a great soul like Ananda, such a state of mind could not have occurred more than once, especially with the Enlightened One as his guide. But, what about ordinary people like me who are prone to such doubts more frequently? Time and again, I feel that I am not reaching anywhere and get tempted to give up the whole idea of spiritual progress and live as I please. When doubts arise, I feel that either I am unfit or that I am doing my *sadhana* wrongly. It is only with great effort of will that I am able to start afresh. Does it happen only to me or is it common? Please tell me what to do when I am in the grip of such a mood again.

Master: This is not a phenomenon peculiar to you. Every sincere aspirant passes through these dark moods; they are the tools that Nature's negative forces use to test the sincerity of the aspirant. Great saints have had these moods. Don't worry; these moods pass. In spiritual terms, this state is called the dark night of the soul.

When such a mood comes, meditate calmly, chant the sacred *Aum* or just relax by listening to beautiful melodious music. Don't take any serious decision. Wait till your mind becomes free of tension. A person who knows the secret of *pranayama* can get over this condition easily.

After the dark night of the soul dawns the clear day and you'll be able to think clearly. Once your mind attains the capacity to experience the spiritual bliss personally and you begin to depend less on what others have taught you and what you have read, and when practical experience replaces theoretical knowledge, all your doubts will vanish and your progress on the spiritual path will accelerate.

Aum Tat Sat

Notes and References

1. Logically, or better linguistically, the term 'reality' must refer to that 'content' which is disclosed in the highest form or quality of our experience, and the experience which discloses that content ceases to be 'human' in any narrow sense of the word.
2. According to Shankara there are three levels of existence: *paramarthika*, corresponding to the Absolute Reality, *Brahman*; *vyavaharika,* apparent reality of our day-to-day world of change; and *pratibhasika*, the illusory world of dreams, hallucination, a wrong sense of perception like mistaking a rope for a snake etc.,
3. The original story, Plato's parable of the cave, is different from the adapted version of my guru but, in essence, Plato's parable also differentiates between what is apparent to our conditioned modes of thinking and sensory perceptions and what lies beyond it—M.
4. Some years later, I came across the following lines in Dr Roger Jones's book *Physics as Metaphor*:
   "Our idolatrous notion of an objective world, independent of our minds is sustained by the qualitative, subjective feel of our senses, corroborated by objective measure. The raw data of my senses is largely **interpreted** by me in terms of a construct of reality based on the measurement of physical properties. I do not see a table. What I see is an oddly-shaped brown area in my visual field. I do not see its height, breadth and width. I infer these by fitting my touch and visual sensations into a predetermined construct for a table which has certain spatial properties with measurable dimensions. I cannot even feel the

table-top or its solidity. I feel only a sensation in my fingers (called pressure) when I try to close them, or an abrupt resistance to my fist swung down before me. These constructs are bolstered by the knowledge that I can measure and, therefore, verify, the table's height, weight, thickness, and so on.

5. The names given to the consciousness in deep sleep is *prajna*, in the waking state *vaishvanara*, and in dream *taijasa*.

   "*Prajna* is a state of knowledge, though the external and internal states are held in abeyance. It is the conceptual self, while the two other ones are the imaginative and perceptual ones."

   Dr S. Radhakrishnan

   Vaishvanara indicates a state common to all men or a state of material condition and *taijasa* is consciousness of the internal or mental state.

6. The practical techniques cannot be given in print or by any other method without the direct personal mediation of the teacher. They have to be learnt from a perfect adept. I was warned by my guru that revealing the techniques, say through books or some other secondary material, would be dangerous to the novice. In his words, "Bear in mind that the *yogi* is playing with forces more powerful than electricity or even atomic energy; a wrong move can physically and mentally wreck him!—'M'.

4

THE ESSENCE OF HINDUISM

The word 'Hinduism' is used here, not in the narrow sense of any 'ism', a creed, a sect. The word itself was coined much later, what is designated by the term existed before; it has greater antiquity than the restrictive prison of a religion, creed or sect. Though for practical purposes we may adhere to this nomenclature, it should not be confused with any institution-bound religion. What Hinduism comprises is a spiritual teaching with its philosophy and metaphysics together with the cultural externals that are added to any such system, the whole forming the *Sanatana Dharma.*[1] No single book, no single topic, no single person has any inalienable claim on Hinduism. Its basis is a vast body of literature starting with the *Vedas*, which have existed almost since the beginning of civilisation. True, there have been additions and explanations by successive sages and teachers, who in their wisdom enriched the *Vedas* rather than distorted them. The *Vedas* themselves have no identifiable author. Though each of the *Vedas* is divided into the *samhitas*, hymnals; *brahmanas*, theological and ritualistic treatises; and the *Upanishads*, philosophical enquiries; it is the *Upanishads* that have unequalled appeal to different people for different reasons at different times.

The reason for this is not far to seek; for, in the words of Deussen, "They are philosophical conceptions unequalled in India or, perhaps, anywhere else in the world." Almost all the philosophical problems are dealt with here. Together with the *Brahma Sutras* or *Vedanta Sutras* of Vyasa and the *Bhagavad Gita*, the *Upanishads* form a triple canon of Hinduism known as the *prasthana traya*. And the *prasthana traya* can be considered as the sum and substance of Hinduism. Though the *prasthana traya* is based on the *Vedas*, it has an independent, unquestionable authority as the final arbiter of Hinduism. Its importance can be gauged by the fact that all the great *acharyas,* whether they were *advaitins* like Shankara, *vishishtadvaitins* like Ramanuja, or *dvaitins* like Madhava, have accepted them as an authority to substantiate and support their own philosophical contentions.

Therefore, when we say the essence of Hinduism, we include all of these together. We also include the *bhakti* literature, we include the *karma yoga* literature which you will find best illustrated in the *Bhagavad Gita*, and what may be called the *jnana marga* literature which is very well represented in the *Upanishads* and the commentaries on these, starting from Gaudapada down. A study of all this literature will give a student a grasp of what is meant by the essence of Hinduism. It is a universal body of literature which any qualified *adhikari*, aspirant, may enquire into. Whether he reaches the goal of his enquiry ultimately or not is a different story. Somebody who is qualified to enquire into it must have the requisite qualifications, which means that he must be very serious and very sincere in his attempt to enquire into the Truth.

It would be useful at this stage to try and get a glimpse of the highest goal to which such an enquiry can lead the sincere aspirant. There are different paths to reach this point. Yet, the goal is one—that of finding out the answer to the basic question posed by the *Kenopanishad*: "Who or what is it that sits behind my eyes and sees through them; what is it that hears when I say 'I heard'; who or what is it that gives my mind the capacity to think; who is that *Deva*, who is that Being, which is responsible for the fact that I say 'I see', 'I hear', 'I think'; what or who is this?" (See also *Quest for Self*, where this is elaborated.) This is a metaphysical question and not a down-to-earth one to be answered by a biodata. The *Upanishadic* enquiry is a deep one, namely, to discover the basic root, the Core of one's Being. The real question is: "Who am I? Am I just a bundle of flesh and bones? Or, am I really the physical body itself? Or, as some occultist would say, 'Am I a subtle body inside a physical body?' Or, am I much deeper, much subtler, than all these things put together? Is there a Being in me which is beyond all the limitations of both the physique and the psyche?"

If one practises some techniques of *yoga*, *tantra*, or *mantra* one may develop some *siddhis*, psychic powers. Though such powers can be acquired, they themselves will not help you to attain *Brahman*. The *Brahman* that the *Upanishads*, the *Bhagavad Gita* and all the other scriptures talk about is beyond any intermediate stages of spiritual development. If the seeker makes whole-hearted and persistent efforts, whether he has obtained any powers or not, he may finally realise this Reality. However, what remains at this stage is not his mind, intellect, or any other commonly acknowledged instrument of cognition but the *Brahman* itself. He is no more a person identifiable with his overt body or actions; he becomes pure Absolute Consciousness.

The *Upanishadic* question is answered in a slightly different manner in the *Bhagavad Gita*. Here, Krishna says: *"Aham Atma Gudakesha, sarva bhutasya sthithah; Aham adis ca madhyam ca bhutanam anta eva ca"* — "I am the Self, the *Atman*, in the hearts of all creatures; the beginning, the middle, and the end of all beings." You will observe a subtle difference in this answer. Whereas the

Brahman, which is the same as the *Atman* of the *Upanishads*, is spoken of as without qualities, *nirguna*, here we find that Krishna, the Lord, appropriates to Himself the term *Atman*. And Krishna is with attributable qualities, *saguna*. Such an apparent difference is well recognised by Vedanta. The *nirguna Brahman* of the *Upanishads* is Absolute Consciousness transcending all states that can be determined or understood by ordinary experience; it cannot be affirmed by reference to anything we are able to experience normally. On the other hand, *saguna Brahman* where *Brahman* is identifiable with a specific God, *Ishta Devata*, has a describable content, namely, the attributes of God; it can be affirmed and something can be said about it. It should, however, be emphasised that the essence of the experience in both the cases is not qualitatively different; though the paths that lead to them are *jnana marga* for the attainment of *nirguna Brahman* and *bhakti marga* for *saguna Brahman.*[2]

If you look at the verse, there is another point that will strike us—Krishna's use of the word *Gudakesa*, conqueror of sleep, as an appellation of Arjuna. In the *Gita*, you will find that, in many places, Krishna calls Arjuna by different names. Sometimes, it is Arjuna; sometimes it is *Kaunteya*; sometimes it is *Gudakesa*; sometimes it is *Nagha*; sometimes, he also says *Mahabaho*, strong-limbed one. There are two reasons for this. One is that, if you examine that particular word, you will find that it is applicable to the content of the verse. Secondly, Krishna is a great psychologist. If you keep telling a person, "You are a stupid fellow" all the time, he will never learn anything. In real life, what happens is that the teacher comes to the class with a big cane in his hand. As soon as he enters, the students start shivering. Then he asks one of the students a question and the latter nervously gives an answer which may be wrong. The teacher immediately says, "You are a stupid fellow." Finished; from that day, the boy or girl concerned doesn't learn anything. The student gives up because he identifies himself with stupidity. In the *Gita*, on the other hand, Krishna gives Arjuna encouragement at every step. When He says *Mahabaho*, he means, "I know you are a strong chap, but that is not everything; there are many things that you have still to learn."

Here, Krishna calls Arjuna *Gudakesa*, which means one who has conquered sleep. Why is Arjuna called one who has conquered sleep? What could be the meaning? That he has insomnia? It is not that. One does not become a great *yogi* by developing sleeplessness. In fact, *yogis* whose minds are very calm are known to go into deep sleep—this is called *yoganidra*—and rest much more than anyone else. If one understands the context in which this name is used, the meaning becomes clear. Here, *Gudakesa* means one who has conquered the darkness of sleep, which is ignorance.

There are two reasons for Krishna's using this form of address. Firstly, he is talking about the possibility of Arjuna ultimately realising the Truth. When this happens and Arjuna enters the superconscious state or *samadhi* even for five or ten minutes, his entire system will get absolutely relaxed—there will be a sort of suspended animation—and every cell of his body will have complete rest. Normal sleep will, therefore, not be necessary for him to rejuvenate himself. Secondly, Vedanta says that we are all in a state of illusion. We have to be careful to understand this statement correctly. There is a tendency to misinterpret it by saying that the world itself is an illusion. The real meaning rather is that we are all suffering from delusions. To wake up from that sleep of delusion is to be free. However, Krishna is fully aware that this state of superconsciousness, which is a state that is different from the consciousness during the waking and dream states, cannot be gained by Arjuna in a short time. When Arjuna ultimately gains this state of superconsciousness, when he finally comes to realise that his inner core is constituted by Krishna Himself—*"Aham adishesha bhutanam anta"*—that "He is the beginning, the middle, and also the end", and that He is also the *Atman* that is inside him, then he could be said to have fully conquered the sleep of ignorance.

There is no crash course available for achieving this goal. One may or may not achieve it. One may achieve it in a short period of *sadhana* or after many years of serious efforts. The well-known story of Shankaracharya and his disciple, Hastamalaka is instructive in this context. When Shankara, whose fame as a philosopher and saint had spread far and wide, was wandering about in South India, he was once taken to a house by the parents of a small boy; they were facing an unusual problem. They said to him, "Please come with us; our boy doesn't talk. From the time he was born, he has not opened his mouth; he just sits there. Perhaps, he is suffering from some disease. We have tried everything; the Ayurvedic physicians have tried their best; nothing improves him. Maybe you could do something to save him." Shankara saw this small boy sitting in a corner. The story goes that he asked him, "Why don't you talk?" and the boy answered, "Of what?" The parents were very happy; this was the first time he had uttered a word. Shankara said, "Whatever you like." The boy replied: "That which is the Truth, no words can describe. And if we express it in words, they cannot be the description of the Truth; so, what shall I say?" Shankara is supposed to have told him, "You are ready; come with me." The boy answered, "I have been waiting for you," and accompanied the sage on his wanderings. Shankara named him Hastamalaka, which means that he had the truth in his palm, *hasta*, as if he was holding the *amalka* fruit in it. There may, therefore, be some exceptional cases like that; one can never say.

To see how this sleep of ignorance can be conquered, let us refer to the *Mandukya Upanishad*. Since the explanation given in it can be found elsewhere in this book, only the salient points are being recapitulated here. This *Upanishad* starts with the description and an explanation of the word *Aum*. First, the theory is discussed and the last few verses explain how this word is to be used for practical purposes to wake up from the sleep of ignorance. *Aum* is divided into three parts, starting with the 'a' which is the basic and simplest sound which every human being utters. So, the chant starts with the 'a', then rolls to the middle of the tongue to utter the sound 'u', after which it travels to the last part for the sound of 'm', where the mouth is closed—*Aum*. After that, if one wants to utter any fresh sound, that is, to **create** a new sound, one has to open his mouth once again. There are many discussions on this word in our various scriptures where the three syllables are identified with creation, preservation, and destruction. However, in the *Mandukya*, this is explained in a slightly different manner. Here, it is said that 'a' represents the waking state of consciousness, the normal state in which all of us function; that the sound 'u' represents the dream state or the *swapna avastha* when we dream; and finally the 'm' represents the state of dreamless deep sleep or *sushupti*. These are the three states of consciousness which are known to everyone.

The *Upanishad* then talks about a fourth state called the *Turiya Avastha*, which really cannot be called a state, because it doesn't resemble any of the three known states of consciousness. *Turiya* transcends the three states of waking, dream, and deep sleep. When we are awake, the dream state is unreal; when we are in the dream state, the waking state is unreal; when we are in deep sleep or *sushupti*, all these states cease to exist. There is absolute non-recognition, nothing is recognised. Yet, when you wake up, you say, "Oh, I had a very deep sleep." This shows that there **has been** a witness to this, but that this witness doesn't remember or is not aware of it during your state of deep sleep. According to the *Mandukya*, *Turiya* is that Witness which exists throughout: in the waking state, in the dream state, as well as in deep sleep. According to the Vedantists, the *yogi* is one who recognises or has come to understand that that Witness which remains unaltered—it is called just *Sakshi*, bare Witness—doesn't get altered by any of the different changes that take place during the waking state, during the dream state, and during deep sleep.

Vedanta says that that Witness is the real you. Normally, you identify yourself with one or the other states of dream, waking, and deep sleep. When the Witness remains unidentified with any of the states, then that is *Tat tvam Asi*, that is, "You are That'. But once this stage is reached—you can't say 'reached' because it is not something to be reached—when that is realised or found, then it remains forever. It is not something that can be found and forgotten. One understands then that this bare Witness remains unaffected through all the three states and is aware of what is going on, but is **not involved** in anything that is happening. It is described in *Vedantic* literature as *Satchidananda*. It is supposed to be *nirguna*, that is, without any qualities. '*Sat*' means that It exists; whatever else exists or does not exist, This exists; whatever existed before but is no more now, It exists. Therefore, *Sat* means the actual Existence. *Chit* means the consciousness of existence. Finally, It is full of *Ananda* or Bliss. Even *tantra* defines the Reality, though *tantra* is generally associated with various strange things. It is true that there are parts of *tantra* which are associated with strange things but there are also other parts which are not. *Tantra* defines the Ultimate Reality as *Anantam Anandam Brahma*, that is, *ananda* which has no end, that endless *ananda*, is *Brahman*. In Vyasa's *Vedanta Sutras*, this *Brahman*, the core of all beings, is described or defined as *'Asti Bhadi Priya'* instead of *Sathidananda*. *Asti* means that It exists—It is there; *Bhadi* means the consciousness, the effulgence, the light; and *Priya* means love, which is very close to *ananda*. These are predominant qualities of the *Brahman* or *Atman,* if you prefer to call it that.

From all the above, which is just a very brief review of the essence of Hinduism, one may jump to the conclusion that it is too theoretical, too metaphysical, to be of any practical use to anybody; that it may be all right to read about in books or to philosophise on, but that it has no practical relevance in our day-to-day lives.

Nothing could be further from the truth. The body of literature called Vedanta is a vast reservoir of all the **actual** experiences of the *rishis* from time immemorial. It is a fund of practical knowledge; it is a reservoir from which any lesson that any particular person wants can be drawn. It is also so infinite that there is no fear that it will ever be exhausted. A possibility exists that new discoveries may still be made in this field and that these will again be added on to the same reservoir. This is a reservoir which is full of the experiences of people who have understood and actually experienced the core of the teachings in different shades and to different degrees. Unlike some theories which cannot be proved by experience, here fortunately is a whole body of literature authored by a line of *rishis* who have themselves experienced what they teach. Each of them has talked to us according to his own bent of mind. Every human being differs from another in aptitude and temperament. That is why we have different paths like *Jnana Yoga, Bhakti Yoga, Raja Yoga,* etc. But if there is one compendium that deals with all various approaches—and, therefore, the essence of Hinduism—it is the *Bhagavad Gita.* Each chapter of this great *vade-mecum* elaborates on a different approach to reach the same goal; every individual can choose the approach which suits him best.

Whether the progress is fast or slow depends on the method adopted by an individual, on his aspirations, on the effort he puts in, and on the path that he follows. Ultimately, however, irrespective of the approach followed, the end result will be the same.[3]

To have a brief idea of one of the practical aspects of Hinduism, let us take recourse to the *Gita*. It sees the human mind as a major stumbling block on the path to Reality, because it can cause untold havoc. What happens to a mind (or intellect) that is severely agitated is described in the following *shloka* of the *Bhagavad Gita*, (Chapter II-*Shloka* 63): *"Dhyayato vishayanpumsaha, sanghasteshupajayate; sanghat sanjayate kamaha kamatkrodho abhijayate; krodhadbhavati sammohaha, sammohat smritivibrahma; smritibrahmashat buddhinasho; buddhinashat pranashyati."* This is a description of the state of an agitated mind. What we require is just the opposite. When your mind is continuously exposed to the five senses and when the senses are constantly in touch with worldly sense objects, an attachment for the latter develops in you. Then, there arises a desire to possess these objects. You cannot keep away entirely from worldly objects, living in the world as you do. Sometimes, when you are unable to acquire or enjoy these, you become frustrated and angry. When you are angry, your reason just doesn't work; you do not think of the pros and cons; you even lose your memory; you forget that you are a father, or a mother, or a wife. It's a sort of madness; every bit of anger, every spell of anger is madness. Such an agitated mind is useless even for such things as investigating a scientific problem or enjoying good music. To perform any activity satisfactorily, you have to employ your whole energy and attention. In order to do this, you require a certain amount of calmness and stability first; an agitated mind cannot go into these things. Anger is also not always immediately expressed. Many unexpressed angers are suppressed inside the psyche and these can cause untold damage in the long run.

You can imagine the state of mind of a person who is constantly exposed to the sensory world and its insidious impact on him. He gets confused and his confusion leads to *smritibrahmah*, loss of memory. Loss of memory, in turn, leads to *buddhinashah*, destruction of intelligence. And then, the whole sequence described above takes place. How can one avoid this? One may well ask, "Shall I cut myself off from all the senses?" That is not possible. This is where the practice of yoga comes in. Krishna tells Arjuna that the basic requisite for a personal experience of the Truth is a state of calmness of the mind; that one cannot start off on the spiritual path until one can sit down and **calmly** take stock of any situation. This is possible only if one has had the necessary training to do it.

All of yoga—particularly *Ashtanga Yoga* or the yoga of eight limbs—provides a practical technique suited for this purpose, although it will be a mistake to say that it will give one a method to reach the Truth. It only lays down a practical technique to concentrate one's mind and energies to reach a state of mental stability from which one can take off on the path of spiritual progress. The great scripture called the *Ashtanga Yoga Sutras* of Patanjali defines yoga as *"Yoga chitta vritti nirodha"*; that is, yoga is the calming of the vibrations of the *chitta*, the mind stuff, which is normally in movement all the time, jumping from one thing to another. *Nirodha* is the stopping of this jumping about of the mind stuff. This is achieved by the practice of yoga.

In order to derive the full benefits of yoga, one has to observe various mental and moral disciplines known as *yama* and *niyama*.[4] At first flush, they may appear irrelevant; on closer inspection, however, you will find them essential to maintain the health of the body and mind. It is only after practising these that one begins to go on to the next stage. However, this doesn't mean that one should first become morally perfect and only then practise yoga; this will never work out. So, one has to go on practising both things side by side. No one can be absolutely perfect and the *rishis* knew that. The absolutely perfect *Jeevanamukta* does not need to practise yoga. So, the very fact that one is trying to practise it means that there are defects in him, that there are vast areas where he can improve. One may trip in the process but he should not give up. Even in worldly pursuits, you try and you fail sometimes; then you try again and you may fail again. Much more perseverance is required here. Therefore, one has to try, try, and try constantly before one achieves the desired state of calmness of mind.

All this is best done under the guidance and encouragement of a teacher. One has also to study the scriptures. This is not the fashion nowadays; so, that is also difficult for the modern man. One should not get discouraged; there is always hope. The *Gita* itself says "*swalpamadyasya dharmasya*", which means that, even if you have practised a little bit, your effort will help you ultimately to cross the *mahato bhayat*, the great fear of rebirth. Hence, to cross the ocean of *samsara*, even a little bit of effort helps. Whatever effort one puts into it is not lost.

You can't use a better expression than that which Swami Vivekananda used when he was talking about the efforts of individuals. He said, "Each soul is potentially divine. This is the essence: each soul is potentially divine. To bring out the divinity in one is the **whole** of yoga." These may not be the exact words that he used but it is the essence of what he said. To bring out this divinity—be it through work or worship, be it through practice of yoga, the study of Vedanta, through *Bhakti*, through *Karma*, it doesn't matter. To bring out this divinity should be the aim of all life. This sums up the essence of Hinduism.

Notes and References

1. Etimologically, *dharma* means 'to hold, have, or maintain'. It is then the form of things as they are and the power to keep them as they are. *Sanatana Dharma* can be loosely translated as eternal law that sustains and governs the universe and all that pertains to it.
2. *Saguna Brahman* is the content of a 'loving' experience of unity; *nirguna Brahman* is the 'content' of an intuitive experience of identity. *Saguna Brahman* is not the highest possible form of experience; nevertheless, it is an extremely valuable experience in that it enables the *advaitin*... to affirm on one level the essential quality of everything that has being.

   -Eliot Deutsch,
   "Advaita Vedanta":
   a Philosophical Reconstruction.

   (This view, of course, is that of the *Advaitins*, practitioners of *jnana marga* like Sri Shankara. The *Bhaktimargis* like Madhava, Ramanuja *et al* contest such a view. The debate needn't bother us if we accept the fact that it is not given to everyone to follow the abstract path of *jnana*, while *bhakti marga* can be followed by all.)
3. The *Gita* is one of the clearest and most comprehensive summaries of the Perennial Philosophy ever to have been made. Hence its enduring value, not only for Indians, but for all mankind. The *Bhagavad Gita* is perhaps the most systematic statement of the Perennial Philosophy.
4. *Yama*, moral/social discipline; *ahimsa*, non-violence; *satya*, truthfulness; *asteya*, non-stealing; *brahmacharya*, celibacy; and *aparigraha*, non-acquisitiveness.

   Niyama, mental, individual discipline; *saucha*, cleanliness; *santosha*, contentment; *tapas*, austerity; *swadhyaya*, self-study; and *Isvara pranidhana*, surrender to God.

   N.B: According to Sage Manu, celibacy does not exclude hygienic sex within matrimony.

5

ILLUSIONS UNDER WHICH WE LIVE

Do we have a clear grasp of the world in general and ourselves in particular or are we under some kind of illusion that we cannot pierce behind to see reality?

For an answer we needn't formulate a new philosophy, nor do we have to depend on any newfangled theories or science. Our own scriptures, especially Vedanta, have given the answer centuries ago—it is encapsulated in the concept of *mayavad*. Unfortunately, at the mention of *mayavad*, the general tendency is to reject it as a metaphysical abstraction, fit only as a subject for the philosopher or the theologian with his head in the clouds. How can Vedanta and its concepts, axioms and theories have any relevance to the modern man who has stopped reaching for the moon and has actually reached there? The answer can be given in two words: "Very relevant". Those who dismiss Vedanta as irrelevant because it is antediluvian are labouring under a fallacy—the fallacy of accepting everything new and rejecting the old. A closer look at Vedanta should clear this false notion.

When we say Vedanta, we are speaking of a whole body of thoughts that has remained the source of wisdom for many a thinker for a very long time; to cite but one, the 19th century philosopher, Schoepenhauer, whose ideas have had great influence, among others, on Freud and Nietzsche. After reading the *Upanishads* (the quintessential literature on Vedanta), he remarked: "How does every line display its firm, definite, and throughout harmonious meaning! From every sentence, deep, original, and sublime thoughts arise, and the whole is pervaded by a high, holy and earnest spirit.... In the whole world, there is no study... so beneficial as that of the *Upanishads*. It has been the science of my life, it will be the solace of my death."

What is found in Vedanta is not a farrago of some half-cooked and indigestible theories by primitive minds; it is a rich mine of truths, including the Absolute Truth that the sages and *rishis* actually experienced, and which can be experienced by others too. If replication of an experiment is the criterion of validity in science, then Vedanta is as much a science as modern physics, biology etc.

The literal meaning of Vedanta can be analysed thus: *Veda-anta*, the end of the *Veda*, the word *Veda* having the meaning of knowledge. The term Vedanta seems to be purposely ambiguous. It may mean the philosophical and psychological sections of the *Vedas* appended to their ends and known as *Upanishads*. It may also mean the end or culmination of all knowledge beyond which there is no more to learn.

The *Upanishads* talk about self-discovery, of understanding one's own self in its various complexities and arriving at the basic source of man and the universe itself. Vedanta is aptly considered to be the end of all knowledge because it goes directly and definitively to the meaning and source of our very existence.

Having stated that, one must not conclude that all that can be said about truth and reality need not be further enquired into. Vedanta itself would discourage such a passive acceptance. For Vedantic enquiry is a continuing process, updated every time in the light of new knowledge and evidence. Therefore, it is essential to look at the concept of Vedantic *mayavad* from our present day perspective. To ensure that our approach is dispassionately impartial, we shall keep the scriptures away for the time being and look into the topic of the essay afresh.

One great illusion all of us live under is that of believing or acting as if our life were eternal. We see death everywhere, every day. Newspapers are full of it. Personally we come to know of many deaths among our kith and kin. Yet we develop a blind spot regarding our own deaths. It is not that we are unaware that we shall die one day; it is only that we act as if we had control over it, that we could call the shots. Therein lies the paradox. We know that death is the only true democrat that treats everyone with equality; yet we function as if we had the magic to fend it off as long as we like. It may appear morbid or unduly pessimistic to rub the motif of death in this manner. Nevertheless, it is the only sure way we can face, fair and square, the irrevocability of our death, thereby dispelling the illusion we are subject to—the illusion of our near-immortality that propels us towards extremes of behaviour and action. The way we cherish this illusion is through hope, which can be the cause as well as the consequence of our illusion.

As an interesting aside, it may be mentioned that our inability to accept death has permeated into our language itself. Whatever language we speak—all languages in all communities—we resort to euphemisms when referring to death, as if it were a taboo that could be wished away by a not-overt mention of it. We say: "He has passed away"; "She has gone to heaven"; "My mother is beyond the veil"; "His father is no more", and so on. Sometimes we even make light of it by humorous expressions like 'Kicked the bucket', 'Handed in the dinner pail', 'Became a cancelled cheque' etc., as if by mocking it, we succeed in extracting death's fangs. Moved by the same fear, people of all climes and times have devised ways of perpetuating the illusion of everlasting life. For example, the Pharaos of Egypt had their bodies preserved as mummies and entombed in palatial pyramids in the hope that they could come to life again. To this day, rituals and ceremonies of all kinds are observed after a death, their purport being not very dissimilar from those of ancient Egypt. This is not to disparage such customs; it is only to wonder whether they are not a way of hoping for the conquest over death.

Isn't it the same kind of hope that makes us live on fantasies for a future that is uncertain? "I shall do this. I shall do that. The house I build will be different from the ones I've lived in until now. My son is going to be a doctor of renown." Aren't these the thoughts that nourish our illusion of a postponed death? "Others may drop dead any time; not me. What if I drink, smoke, and lead a dissolute life? I am as strong as an ox and nothing can kill me in a hurry." So run our incorrigible hopes. No doubt, man cannot live without hope, and hope means an expectation in or of a future. This is perfectly all right, understandable; for it makes life, as we know it, worth living. It is the same 'worth' this essay proposes to assess and revalue; not so much to devalue it as to weigh it in a proper balance.

Closely allied to the illusion of a postponed death is the illusion of lasting happiness. Each one of us thinks: "If I win a lottery of a few hundred thousands, I shall be happy." (If you try to convince the person that it is a mere gamble and, that even if he wins it, he may not be happy, he is more apt to attribute it to your jealousy or ill-will than to your reason.) So is our illusion about possessions. For example, "If my health is perfectly all right, I will be happy." The unmarried man thinks, "If I get married, I'll be very happy"; the married man on the other hand thinks, "Oh my God! If I had only remained a bachelor, I would have been happy." We do not realise that these are all hopes and will often remain hopes till the end. The desire in us for happiness is such that we like to think that, by gaining something physically or having something in our possession, we would be very, very happy. All our lives are spent in trying to achieve or get that particular thing, so that we can attain the happiness that we desire; we never really achieve this elusive end.

Take another example. You don't have a house. You are very unhappy because you think everybody else you know has a house; so, you must have a house too. You work hard, you save, you beg, borrow and steal to build a house. Or, if you have a lot of money, you invest a chunk of it in a house project. Once you have it, you begin to feel, "This is a dead asset; why did I put all my money into it? If I had put it in business, I could have made more money." So, the happiness which you thought is going to be absolute by having a house of your own is already beginning to fade a little. Then a thought arises, "I have to go to Delhi on business or I want to go somewhere on holiday for a month. When I had no house, I would have gone without a second thought. Now, I have to lock it up and, even then, thieves may break in. When I come back, only the house may be standing there!" Hence, once you get hold of the object which you wanted, the happiness which you thought it would bring you slowly begins to fade. You begin to feel "The ideal situation is something else; this is not it." This search for the ideal situation in which one can be permanently happy continues. The search, alas, never ends!

There is also another aspect involved in this. Suppose you do become happy with something which you get. You are very happy with it for a while. After some time, doubts assail you. You are afraid that it may be snatched away; that it may be destroyed on its own. Even if there is no physical destruction or disappearance of your possession, you may still be unhappy; for, something else has taken its place as more worthy of bringing you happiness. (Strangely enough, the only thought that doesn't bother us at our time of joy in our possession is that death itself may snatch that object away from us. All of us shut that possibility out altogether.) Thus we have seen that no sooner we achieve a state of happiness, than that state begins to slip out of our fingers. We then want to hold on to it; we direct all our energies to this effort to hold on to it. If one is holding on to something, afraid all the time that it will slip out of one's fingers, then how can there be happiness? If that fear is always there, how can one be tranquil or happy? Of course, we don't like to think about this.

The alternative to that fear is a hope of freezing that moment of happiness for all time to come; the hope that, after we achieve whatever we set out to achieve, our enjoyment of it is one of continuity. Unfortunately, time has other views; it is not static; it cannot be checked or stopped. You will be going against the inexorable laws of time, running against time, if you hope that your happiness will remain unaltered. This hope will never be fulfilled. For example, somebody is a little overweight. He realises that it is not the fashion to be overweight. Besides, extra weight can lead to diseases. So, he wants to reduce his weight. He achieves this. He is happy till a closer look in the mirror shows the tell-tale marks of time—a wrinkle here and there, a few grey hairs, a coarseness of skin. Modern beauty aids and treatment can, of course, camouflage the etchings of time for a while. But for how long?

Without belabouring with further examples, one can say, without fear of contradiction, that everything changes over a period of time. Our happiness, on the other hand, depends on things that we have achieved remaining as they are without changing, or our state of happiness remaining unaltered, or our own death a postponed possibility.

From the foregoing statements—perhaps, yes perhaps, with an undertone of pessimism—it needn't be concluded that there is nothing worth living for, and that, therefore, there is no need for any activity. You will soon realise that you will not succeed in doing this also. Nature is such that you will be forced to do something or the other all the time. You cannot stop doing everything altogether unless you are terribly lazy, in a coma, or in a drug-induced stupor. "Agreed; material possessions and social positions may not last long but surely there is happiness in personal relations," you may demur. This again is an illusion. Everyone of us believes, unless he is a total misanthrope, that someone or the other loves him. The facts prove otherwise. Today, you have money or position or power and everybody seems to love you. Tomorrow, you may not have money and nobody will love you. Once you lose either—sometimes, even without any such loss but being momentarily or physically dependent—you will find that the love and respect you 'commanded' (an apt word) take on a different colour. The following story will illustrate the point.

There was a disciple who told his guru one day, "Sir, I am prepared to give up everything in my life and come away with you to seek spiritual perfection but there is only one thing that stops me. At home my wife, my children, my mother, my father, my uncle, all these people love me so much. How can I leave them and come away? This is the only obstacle." The guru told him, "Fine. If everybody loves you, you should not leave your home. However, let us find out whether this is true by a small experiment. I shall give you two tablets. I will keep one and you keep the other. Take this tablet and go home. Lie down on your bed and swallow this tablet. What will happen is that, to all intents and purposes, anybody who looks at you will think that you are dead. Don't fear; you won't be dead; you'll only appear to be so. And you will be aware of everything that is happening around you. I'll come after some time disguised as a *vaidya*. Then watch the drama and we will talk about your problem afterwards."

So, the man went home and said, "I am not feeling well at all." Everyone gathered around him. He lay down quietly and popped the tablet into his mouth; soon, he had the immobility of death. People started crying including his elderly parents and uncle. Everyone was saying, "Why did you leave us? Instead of you, one of us could have been taken away." The air was rent with lamentations appropriate in a house of the dead. Soon, the teacher arrived. He asked, "What happened?" Words choked by sobs came out of the throng of grieving relatives, "He is dead. He has been so dear to all of us. We wish we were dead, not he." The teacher who had come there pretending to be a *vaidya* consoled them, "Don't cry. I shall bring him back to life with my magic pill." A sudden rush of expectation ran through the gathering. They chorused in hopeful joy, "Please give it to him immediately. You are our saviour." The fake *vaidya* then told them, "Yes, I'll do that. But there is a slight hitch. The magic pill will only be effective if someone volunteers to die in his place. However, I don't fear any lack of volunteers since all of you love him so much. Now, the man who loves him most may lie next to him, ready to die, and I shall revive this man immediately." The hush that followed the *vaidya's* words was as deafening as the wailing before. None came forward to resurrect the 'dearest', who was lying there, aware of all the happenings around him. The guru then put the tablet into the man's mouth and tapped him on his shoulder. He asked, "What do you say now? Are you ready to come with me?" For an answer, the man got up and followed his guru, thoroughly enlightened about his illusion of love.

The purport of the story is not to cast a shadow on 'love' as such; nor is it to exhort renunciation. No, I am not preaching the need for *sanyasa*. I am not a *sanyasi* myself; I am a householder. I am just asking you to look at a fact of life squarely. There are rare people who have concern for others but that concern is different. Normally the people who we think are near and dear to us do not have this type of concern. They may have some biological attachments or conditioned—genetically, psychologically, or socially—belief in maintaining or professing such attachments. Nobody is really attached to anybody else. There may be many reasons for this but this is not the place to go into these.

Now let us also consider the psychological illusions which we live under. You have known someone as a friend for a long time. Your experiences about him have helped you form an image about him. He also has an image about you from his experience. This is normal and is as it should be. The problem crops up in the act of communication. Are we really looking at and communicating with each other or is it the images which do so? Or, if the images are not communicating with each other, is there some other form of communication taking place which does not depend on these images? One has to look at this very carefully because what is really happening is not self-evident. If you consider it from this angle, you will soon discover that, most of the time, the communication between people is not really between people as they really are but between such images. Therefore, there is really no chance of anything new cropping up because the images that we have in our minds are generally very old. In short, communication becomes a reflex behaviour. When you married your wife, you had formed an image about her at that time. Fifteen years later, you are probably still continuing with that image. The same may be the case with her also.

Therefore, there is no real communication between the two of you. Meanwhile, time, the great changer has been at work. Many changes must have taken place and must be taking place in both. We don't give scope or express or understand such changes; we are stuck with our old images without giving them any leeway for change. Yet, we think and act as if we understood each other and blame each other for the altered state. Isn't that an illusion?

Let us go a bit further.

When Vedanta says "Look at yourself; find out about yourself," we generally come to a quick conclusion. We say "We know what we are." This is as much an illusion as we have of others. Finding out about yourself means examining yourself thoroughly in all aspects, what you really are, how you relate to others, and so on and so forth. Unless and until you understand where exactly you are in the changing circumstances, you cannot really make any progress. Otherwise, you will be like a man who is heading towards an unknown destination without first finding his bearings—he may go east instead of west where his destination is if he has no precise clue about his own starting point. In this context, the words of Samuel Foote, the 18th century wit, seem to be apt. He said that he climbed on his horse and rode in different directions all at once.

Now, let us consider another illusion which is very important and which is closely linked to the question of knowledge.[1] A well-known statement in the *Ishavasya Upanishad* is: "He who worships ignorance enters into darkness." That is very clear. Everyone thinks so highly of knowledge that this statement is easily understood. We, therefore, applaud it. But then the *rishi* posits a paradox. He says "And he who worships knowledge enters into greater darkness." How can this be? It takes time to understand and appreciate the significance of the paradox. We cannot accept knowledge as something that leads us to darkness, leave alone into greater darkness. If at all we know anything, isn't it through the knowledge we have acquired? There can be no evolution without gathering knowledge. There is no doubt about this. One has, so to say, to read between the lines to comprehend the paradox posed by the *Upanishad*. What the *rishi* declares is that one enters into greater darkness when he worships knowledge *per se*. If we go a little deeper and look into the essential meaning of this statement, we come to the conclusion that it is knowledge itself that is responsible for the problem. What the *rishi* means is that the true understanding of the subject of enquiry in the *Upanishads*, which is the Supreme Self or the Supreme Being or the Supreme Truth, is not something which can be obtained by acquiring more of what is normally called knowledge.

The reason for this is that all knowledge is contained within the confines of the mind which includes the brain. Now, the *Kena Upanishad*, one of the oldest of the *Upanishads*, declares: *Yanmanasa na manute yenahur mano matam / taddeva Brahma tvam viddhi nedam yadidamupasate;* that is, "That which the mind cannot reach, cannot touch, or cannot conceive of, that alone is *Brahman*, that alone is the Truth, understand that." The Supreme Self, that *Brahman*, is the subject matter of the whole *Upanishidic* enquiry. Therefore, the *rishis* have declared that, to understand that, none of the known different branches of knowledge can be used. If you look carefully into what we normally call knowledge, you will find that this is only memory. On the other hand, the Reality or the True Self is something which cannot be a memory. It is something which is always present, at this moment, here and now.

When I say knowledge, what does it mean? I have previously no knowledge of something. I then apply my mind to it; I try to understand it. The moment I understand it, it is stored away in my brain as a memory. So, when I say I have a knowledge of something, it means that I have a memory of something that I have studied. The acquisition of all knowledge goes through this process. Every bit of knowledge that we have is a memory stored in the brain. And a memory is not a thing of the present; it is a thing of the past. You cannot think of a present memory; all memories are of the past. So, any knowledge that you have is not knowledge of the *Brahman*. Because *Brahman* is ever fresh; it remains with one now, at this moment, right now. But we persist in our illusion about knowledge as we understand it and raise it to a high pedestal for worship.

Again, the *Kena Upanishad* destroys this illusion by the declaration: "He who thinks he knows does not know, and he who does not know knows." This means that, if anybody thinks that he can understand the Reality behind the illusions through knowledge, he does not know. The attempt to reach out for the Truth is so unlike our reaching out for sensory things that it is a totally different process. It is actually not a reaching out but settling down. Again, it is necessary to remember that settling down is not physical act, although the meaning of the word *shad* in *Upanishad* means to sit. Sitting, of course, indicates that you are settling down to think, because if you stand up, you are preparing to move on. But it also means the 'sitting' or settling down of the mind, not a reaching out but settling down. And this settling down can take place only in total tranquillity when all distractions are eliminated. The first thing we have to understand is where we stand at the moment. And when we carefully look at where we stand, we discover that we labour under a hundred thousand illusions which keep us entrapped most of the time. This is what is called *maya*. This trap that we are caught in makes us go round and round in circles. Sometimes, the circle is small, sometimes it is big, but we are always within the circle.

How does one get out of this circle? One cannot reach out and escape. When one understands this correctly, properly, fully, then there is a hope for being free from this cycle. There is no technique that will indubitably help you to achieve your aim. All available techniques are only guide-posts. They can show you the way but you have to do the walking yourself. However, most of the techniques have one feature in common—they are intended to help to keep the mind free from distractions, to bring all the energies together to a focal point. The kind of energy required for such an effort cannot be collected or processed by a distracted mind. So, all *yogic* disciplines are designed to free our minds from distractions, to gather all the energies and bring them to bear in a single-pointed manner on the central question of discovering oneself.

The way of doing this is by achieving calmness and tranquillity of the mind. The mind is a collection of thoughts. Our essence, as Supreme Being or the *Atman*, which the spiritual seeker wants to understand, discover, communicate with, or realise, is beyond this closed circuit of thought. Remaining in this circuit of thought, one cannot touch the Supreme Being. However, to see that thought does not interfere in any way with your realising of the Supreme Being is not so easily achieved. Because the very moment you think, "I want to get rid of thought", you are already thinking. And, when you are thinking, you are again caught in the same cycle. So, is there a way of doing it?

One way of coming to grips with this problem is to watch your thoughts constantly as they occur, to be constantly aware of your thoughts. If you watch your thoughts like this all the time, you will find out where they spring from. And, once you find out the source of your thoughts, there is some chance of your getting free of them. There is no standard technique for achieving this; it is entirely an individual matter. But once you are free of your thoughts, then your job is done. I can also put it this way. Even when you are sitting quietly, the mind ceaselessly keeps on chattering. When the chattering ends, there is silence. This silence is not the same silence which you feel when there is no sound outside. This kind of silence when the chattering of the mind ceases can exist even when the whole din of the marketplace is around you. This din makes no difference to this silence. But, to get to that stage, to observe, and to be aware of your mind and thoughts all the time, it is good to start in a place where there is no sound. Once you have achieved that stage of silence, it doesn't matter where you are. That silence will always be with you.

Indeed, such a course may not suit everyone's nature. There are those who are constantly active physically, either by nature or by external compulsion. The best method for them is to make their work itself a form of *sadhana*. Sincere, dedicated, single-pointed work is a form of worship or *sadhana* when one's desire for spiritual evolution is strong and one wants to be free of the bondage of worldliness. If a person feels that he is bound and wants to be free, such a person can adopt sincere dedicated work oriented towards true evolution as his *sadhana*. Such work is also meditation. Meditation is a process; so it is also work. Obviously, work doesn't mean just physical labour but can mean other things also. Whether he is at the farm or in the office, if a person puts his whole energy into his efforts, then he has already mastered the art of concentration and he is meditating. If he is able to do this, he can apply it to any sphere, spiritual or material.

I can illustrate this with a story. You may have heard of the great Bodhidharma who took what later became Zen Buddhism to China. He was once in his hermitage on top of a hill. Two young gentlemen went to him and said, "We have come a long way to meet you. We are looking for *Satori* (spiritual enlightenment in Zen philosophy). We have heard that you are the person who can guide us." Bodhidharma was drinking his broth. He said, "I am drinking my broth." So, they waited for some time. Then, they again asked him for guidance saying, "We have come here a long way and with great difficulty." He said, "I am drinking my broth." Then he called somebody and said, "Give them some broth." So, they were also provided with bowls of broth. While drinking their broth, they again asked him the same question for the third time. He said, "I am drinking my broth." So, they got quite upset. They said, "We are also drinking our broth." He said, "No. You are drinking your broth and thinking of *Satori*. When I am drinking my broth, I am drinking my broth; therefore, I am in *Satori*." Obviously, he was the one who had mastered the art of putting his whole energy into what he was doing without giving in to distractions of any kind.

6

VEDANTIC QUEST FOR THE TRUE SELF

The quest for the true self, according to Vedanta, is not so much a search for God as for one's own self or inner identity. This automatically implies that we do not know what we really are. Everyone knows what his name is, who he is in society, and he generally allots to himself unconsciously a personality. Contrary to this 'commonsensical' view, our scriptures, especially Vedanta, teach us that there is a being inside each one of us which is different from his external appearance. This is different from the sum total of the image that one has of himself and the image that others have of him. This self is not what is normally meant in usages like 'selfish'. When a person is spoken of as selfish, it is in no way complementary. On the contrary, it is a disparaging term applied to one who sets himself above all and everything. In Western philosophy, there is a view of the self that is known as solipsism; this is an extreme form of scepticism, which denies an external physical world as well as any other minds; it views Self as all that exists or all that can be known.

Far from this is the view of the Vedantist who avers that the Self is one's essential being and that it is not different from any other self. That is to say, our separate, private, individuality is a manifestation of the one all-pervasive, universal Self. The self, limited by or identified with a separate individuality, is not the Self of the Vedantist.

How has this wrong identification come about? When you are a small child, you have a certain identity. As you grow up and become a student, your identity changes. In youth, you are not what you were before. When you have become a family man, you seem to be totally different from the carefree person of your bachelor days. Of course, there may be some basic characteristics common to your continually changing personality. But even these basic characteristics are accidental and can be different, depending on where you were born or to whom you were born (e.g., racial difference to name one basic characteristic). What the *rishis* say is that, beyond all this, there is one common factor that is independent of all external manifestations of a person.

Interestingly, the word personality is derived from the Greek word 'persona', which means a mask. The Vedantic quest is not for the persona, not for the mask, not for the personality that may be a saint at one time and a sinner at another. What Vedanta is looking for is the inner consciousness which is behind the outer personality. The first clarification which Vedanta therefore seeks is this: "Is there really such a consciousness at the core of one, which has no separate identity and which is unaltered by the superficial changes due to birth, nurturing, and growth?"

To find this out, Vedanta looks at the different states of consciousness with which all of us function. Since this topic has been discussed in the chapter *Thus Spake the Master,* I shall confine myself here to a brief recapitulation of the three normal states of wakefulness, dream, and deep sleep. Each of these states is real only as long as it lasts; in other words, the reality of the three states is dependent or contingent on their duration. We have also seen the quandary of King Janaka who wondered whether he was a beggar which he saw himself as during a dream or whether he was really a king. His preceptor, the sage Yajnvalkya, clarified his confusion by assigning to the three states only a relative reality. "What", the king then wanted to know, "was the constant entity that went through the three states and, since it remained constant, was it the real Self?" The answer to this question as given in the *Mandukya Upanishad* has been discussed in detail in the chapter referred to earlier. And that answer, we recall, is that the Self, which acts as a Witness, *Sakshi*, to all the three states and is unalterable is that Absolute Consciousness—the *Brahman*—which transcends everything that is knowable by a reasoning intellect, sensory experience or any other mode of normal cognition. It can be expressed only by an oxymoron—the figure of speech in which apparently contradictory terms appear in conjunction (e.g., bitter-sweet, cruel to be kind, etc.). Thus, it is an experience without being experienced in categoric terms.

The Vedantist's quest is a quest for the Self behind the persona, behind the different masks that the Self wears in the ordinary course of life in the world. We are again and again warned in our scriptures not to mistake the persona for the Self which remains the same in all. Our separate divided selves—call it personalities, individualities, or what you will—can be compared to the different roles an actor takes up on different occasions. If he is a good actor in the specific play he is cast, he acts out the character assigned to him to the best of his histrionic ability. In another play, he is equally capable of a realistic portrayal of a completely different character. However, if he completely forgets that he is only playing a role while acting a particular role, it can lead to serious consequences. Suppose his role is that of a serial killer who strangles his victims. Imagine the consequences of his total identification with that character! (I am told that there are artists known as 'method actors', who so integrally identify themselves with a specific role that they invariably have to be treated by a psychiatrist to help them regain their real-life role. Whether or not this is a hype to promote a particular actor in an attempt to increase his rating as the best is a moot point. What is relevant is the possibility of such an occurrence.)

A beautiful short story 'Who am I this time?' by the American writer, Kurt Vonnegut Jr., can be taken as an extended metaphor for the condition of modern man who mistakes shadow for substance and unreality for reality. Harry Nash, when he is not taking part in plays staged in his small town, is a shy, reserved, colourless person who is so self-effacing that he is invisible in a crowd. But, give him a role and he is transformed. He becomes the character, aggressively violent, rollickingly funny, pathetically morbid, or any other personality that the play demands. Away from the footlights he is a nobody—unnoticed, unrecognised, unapplauded, and worst of all, unsought by both friends and relations.

Then, love is thrust on him unwillingly. A beautiful girl, Helene, who acts with him as the heroine in a play, falls in love with him, mistaking him for what he is not. Despite the warnings from her well-wishers about his off-stage nature, she manipulates him to marry her. The entire small town where they live is agog to know how their married life is working out. Against the general presentiment of a marriage that none expected to last over a few hours, the young wife Helene, seems to be of a cheerful mien that hints of a successful marriage even after three months of her new state. The town is amazed at the miracle.

The secret of their success as man and wife is out when one of Harry's play directors visits them at home.

Harry has just come in from work—as shy and colourless as ever—and is too timid to acknowledge the director's presence. With his head bowed down in an unnameable embarrassment, he weakly whispers, "Who am I this time?" Without a word, Helene thrusts a book at him, picks up another copy of the book herself, and begins to read aloud words of a lovelorn lass. Presto! Harry is transformed unrecognisably—he is now the ardent lover. The director slides away with the knowledge of how Helene has cleverly preserved her marriage.

In a way, are we not all like Harry? We become the role we play on the world's stage, forgetting who we truly are. The search for the Self in Vedanta is the search for the real 'who' behind all the masks.

Another story, a true one now, concerns the sage of Tiruvannamalai, Ramana Maharshi, and it underscores the obstacle to understanding the true Self. When the great *Kavyakanta* Ganapati Shastri went to Ramana Maharshi, he had already gone through the whole gamut of Vedanta. There was nothing more he had to learn in this subject. On his first visit, he was not impressed by the Maharshi. On a second visit, he sat looking at the saint for a long time, wondering what it was that made the saint live his knowledge, while he himself was as ignorant as he was when he began the study. Sitting there looking at the saint, he thought to himself this time, "What is this? I suddenly get the feeling that he knows and I don't." So, he asked him, "Sir, I am not sure but I think you have the answer. I have studied Vedanta, I have gone through everything, and I haven't found the Reality, the true Self. I know it because Vedanta says that, when one knows the true Self, one is free. I know that I am not free; hence, I know that I have not found the true Self. What should I do?" The Maharshi is reported to have kept absolutely quiet for fifteen minutes, just looking at him, without uttering a single word. Then he said, "Actually, I wish we could both just keep silent. But, since you have asked me, let me tell you. Find out the source from where the 'I' has come. All your problems will be solved."

At another time, some other learned *pandit* put a similar question to Ramana. The man started off by saying: "I did this, I did that; I am doing this, I am doing that; I have learnt this, I have learnt that" etc. Then he asked Ramana what he should now do to learn about the true Self. Ramana told him to go back the way he had come. Saying this, the sage walked out of the room leaving behind a piqued and confused man. It was *Kavyakanta* Ganapathy Shastri who then pacified the distraught scholar and told him that what the sage really meant by his statement was that he should not talk so much about himself and his achievements. He advised him never to talk to Ramana of the many things that he had done. One person may say, "I am responsible for everything; I am the biggest man" and so on; another, "I am the smallest man; I am the lowest of the low," etc. Both are excusing themselves from understanding the Reality by saying that one is either too full of power or too powerless to understand It. Such statements are all obstacles to understanding the true Self.

This search for the true Self is what has been discussed in the *Upanishads* from time immemorial and is the only enquiry worthy of consideration by any serious *sadhak*. One of the *Upanishads*, the *Kena Upanishad*, begins with the question: *Keneshitam patati prashitam manah/ kenah pranah prathamah praiti yuktah/ keneshitam vachamimaam vadanti/ chaksuh, shrotram, ka u Deva yunakti*. This can be broadly translated as follows: "Which is this Consciousness or Self, who is this God, who hears when we hear, who sees when we see, who listens when we listen, who thinks when we think?" The student who puts this question has studied other Vedantic scriptures and has already learnt intellectually that he should not identify himself with the personality which he normally tends to identify himself with. The *rishi* answers: "*Yanmanasana manute*, that which the mind cannot conceive of; *yenahur mano matam*, but because of which the mind has the capacity to think; *taddeva Brahma*, that alone is *Brahman*; *tvam viddhi*, please understand this; *nedam yadidam upasate*, nothing that you worship or adore here."

The same *rishi* continues his discussion at a later stage: "This true Self cannot be reached by the eye, *na tatra chaksur gacchati.*" The *sadhak* may think, 'Fine; this I can understand. There are many things that I can't see with my eyes but I know that they exist all the same.' The *rishi* goes on to say, "This Self is something which is indescribable in words, *na vag gacchati.*" The student may then think, 'That is also understandable. There are many emotions which I cannot describe however hard I may try.' Finally, the *rishi* ends up by saying, "The mind also cannot reach it, *na manah.*" The student may now come to the conclusion that this is the height of nihilism. The mind, which includes his brain and his power of thinking, is the highest faculty that he possesses. If he cannot reach the Self even with that, what is he to do now? The question that may arise in his mind at that stage is, "Is there **at all** a way of finding this true Self?"

The pupil engaged in this dialectical enquiry is not an ordinary student; he is an *adhikari*, a student fit for the instruction, one who has the grit and high moral stamina to devote his whole life to the true understanding of life and its rebuilding on the firm foundation of the highest truths of philosophy. Unwilling to attribute nihilism as a tenable interpretation of the teacher's words, he may conclude that the Self which is infinite may never be found, merely because man himself is a finite being. If such a man's finite mind can find and grasp something infinite like this, then the Self cannot remain infinite any longer. Some others may conclude that there is no point in their studying Vedanta any further. Others still may even jump to the conclusion that there is no use undertaking such a search for the Self since a dead end seems to have been reached.

However, the **persistent** *sadhak* knows that this is not the case. For example, he knows that he sees everything with his eyes but cannot see his own eyes; yet, he cannot deny their existence. He knows also that, without his consciousness being present, his eyes are useless. He is aware that people have been studying the Vedanta for hundreds of years. They were certainly not fools. At least a few of them must have discovered that **there IS a way** of finding the true Self. A practical aspect of Vedanta must therefore be in existence which he will now have to investigate and practise. Meanwhile, the *rishi* has continued to explain what he wants to say in words and increasingly gets the feeling that he is not getting anywhere. Therefore, he finally throws up his hands and says, *"Na vidmo na vijanimo yathaitadanusisyat"*; that is, "I really don't know how I am going to teach you this."

It is very difficult to find a **precise** explanation for this situation because we are dealing with something that the *rishis* themselves declare as indescribable in words, *na vag gacchati*. The mind, however much it expands and gets refined, can only operate in the three dimensions in which the physical world operates, viz., length, breadth, and height or depth. Normal human beings cannot therefore conceive of a fourth dimension. In the chapter 'Thus Spake the Master', the analogical example of imaginary creatures with a two-dimensional orientation has already been given. To recapitulate, two wafer-thin creatures, alike in all respects except in their colour, and accustomed to and aware of only the dimensions of their horizontal movements (length and breadth) within their respective containers, are interchanged. Now, one red creature finds itself among the green ones, one green creature among the red. Extending the analogy, let us suppose that both of them have become aware that a cross-over from one container to the other is possible. However, neither of them would be able to explain its experience to its respective companions. The plight of the *rishi* can be compared to that of these two imaginary creatures. He knows that it is **indeed possible** for one or more of his students to achieve Self-realisation, but he cannot explain to them in precise language how they can achieve this.

It is generally people with an intellectual predilection who take to the study of Vedanta. Yet, in spite of the most strenuous efforts that he may put in, the intellectual is most often the very individual who does not achieve success in realising the true Self. This is because he cannot often grasp the fundamentals of the process by which he may be able to do this. He tries his best to study Vedantic theory and to understand and assimilate it. He knows that he can only achieve Self-realisation by meditating and quietening the restless wandering of his mind. Therefore, he even goes through the whole process of intense *sadhana* that is prescribed by Vedanta. But he fails to realise that all this can take him up to only a certain stage of the process. He fails to appreciate that trying to grasp something which he has read about will only yield a projection of his own mind and not the true Self that he is seeking.

It is only when he finally realises ***definitely, deeply, seriously*** *that, even though the mind operates only because of the Self, it is entirely different from the Self, that he may succeed in his attempt.* His mind then stops moving in any direction—this side, that side, or even towards the Self—when he is meditating. If this stage is reached, it may finally settle down completely and become **absolutely quiet**. When this happens, since the mind itself is something made up only of thoughts, it has obviously ceased to exist and has disappeared completely. It must be realised that the *sadhak* cannot reach this stage by conscious effort. He can only create the right conditions for this to happen. When it will occur is also not known. It can only be **observed** when and if it does occur. This is all extremely complicated and difficult to explain or to understand. That is why the *Gayatri Mantra*, the most potent of the Vedantic prayers, does not ask for health, wealth, or things like that. It says instead: "*Dhiyoyonah prachodayat*, clarify, stimulate, illumine my intellect, and make it subtler than it is at present."

When a *sadhak* has achieved a certain quietude of the mind, he may think that he has reached the Self. Of course, he is on the right path, but to achieve Self-realisation is a totally different thing. This happens only when the *sadhak* has reached the stage when his limited mind has totally disappeared. It is only then that the Self appears to him in all Its effulgent glory. But he cannot really describe his experience in words. All the descriptions that have been given of this phenomenon are stepped-down descriptions. Nobody can describe the Self as It was when the *sadhak* was in that stage, because whatever is being explained later is through his mind which was non-existent at that moment. This stage of a thought-free mind is also not one which he has achieved by voluntary effort. It is due to his mind becoming quiet **all by itself**. All the *sadhana* that he has performed, the *japa*, the meditation, etc., is something that clears up his passages and his mind 'to leave the doors and windows open', so to say, 'and to keep the place free from dust and dirt'. Beyond that, he cannot do anything.

If the window is open, the breeze will certainly come; there[1] is no doubt about it. But he cannot dictate to it to come. When It will come also, nobody can say. It comes by Itself uninvited. Of course, he can invite It to come but, if he does this, he may jump to the wrong conclusion that It has come because he has invited It. He can only make sure that, by his *sadhana*, he has 'kept his door and windows open'. This Self which is the basic consciousness behind every individual has, according to Vedanta, no differentiations such as this and that or you and me. To discover and realise It is the whole **aim** of Vedanta. The

process of achieving this is by meditation and observation. Until he grasps that this Self is realised only when his mind is **absolutely quiet and free of thought**, the *sadhak* should continue his *sadhana* because he has still NOT achieved Self-realisation. Only when this happens will he fully understand that this Self is not the self which up to then he has identified himself with, and which is happy when something good happens and unhappy when something bad occurs. He will understand that this Self is always full of bliss; It is the fourth state of consciousness, the *Turiya*, which is the witness of all the other three states. This is not affected by any of the things happening in them and **always** remains pure by itself.

What are the characteristics of one having attained that Self? A person who has attained that Self is one who is always immersed in the bliss of the *Brahman*, *Brahmanandam parama sukhadam*; who is full of that state of pure awareness, *kewalam jnanmurtim*. He is constantly aware of the happiness in his mind. This is a state which does not have any opposites, no two poles, *dandwa teetam*. A person in this state is not upset when something goes wrong. Nor is he excessively exuberant when things go his way. He has also understood that that Self which is in him is the same Self which is in everyone else, *tatwamasyadilakshyam*. It is the only thing, *ekam*, that is eternal, *nityam*. It is *vimalam*; that is, there is no *mala* or impurity of any kind in it. It is also absolutely motionless, *achalam*. Therefore, to understand and experience it, the mind has also to be *achala*, without any movement. It is the witness of everything that is happening, *sarvadhee sakshibhutam*. There are no fickle moods in it, *bhava teetam*. A person who has developed such awareness by proper *sadhana* is not angry at one moment, affectionate at another, and full of hatred a moment later. He is also *triguna rahitam*.[2]

The seeker begins meditating with ten minutes of sitting quietly somewhere and developing an awareness of his thoughts. With enough practice, this can become so natural that he is aware of his feelings, aware of his thoughts **at every moment.** He is constantly aware of where his mind is going at every moment; how his ego is growing stronger day by day; how pride enters and makes him imagine that he is better than all others. All these things are **constantly watched** by him. This is true meditation and he can then be said to be in **perpetual** meditation, not merely when he sits down for the sessions of meditation which he undertakes for short periods every day. No doubt such daily practice is also necessary and important. But it is only through **constant awareness** that the Self can be reached.

More than anything, he must be persistent in pursuing the path of Vedantic *sadhana*; he has to take courage and not get bogged down by difficulties. Obstacles will always be there in the path of the sincere seeker of Truth. If one takes two or three falls and admits defeat, then the race will be over. It is the one who falls down but who stands up again and goes forward bravely who finally breasts the tape. That is why the *Upanishad* declares: *Nayan Atma balahi neha labhya*; that is, "This *Atman* is not attainable by the weak." This was a favourite slogan of Swami Vivekananda. What is hinted at by 'strong' in this context is the courage, the enterprise, and the energy required for this type of spiritual *sadhana*. To obtain this energy, the intelligent *sadhak* should ensure that his energies are not dissipated in useless activities. Activity cannot be avoided by anybody. But people often indulge in very many activities which are useless in this effort to reach the Truth.

How does one know that some activity he is indulging in is useless for this purpose? He can discover this only if he develops his awareness. He will then be able to sit down and think: "What are the activities that I normally indulge in which are really useful for me to reach my goal and what are those that are just actions of habit?" Such habitual actions may be harmless by themselves, say for example, going to the club for a game of cards. Some others may be harmful, like indulgence in gambling and illicit sex as a matter of habit. What is important from the spiritual point of view is that one should be aware of what an action of habit is and what activity is really beneficial to one.

(The preceding essay is based on one of my talks. Since the talk elicited some important questions pertaining to the topic, they are added on here—M.)

QUESTIONS AND ANSWERS:

Q.1. *Are there any signs, psychological or otherwise, by which a seeker may find out, at least for himself, whether he is progressing on the right path?*

M: This is a very relevant question. I can appreciate that a spiritual aspirant would like to know the answer to the above question in the earlier stages of his quest. One of the most important symptoms or signs is that one becomes less and less self-concerned—I am referring to the smaller self now, not to the real Self. As one progresses on the path, one actually begins to see the presence of the real Self even vaguely—may not be very definitely—but vaguely in other persons. Therefore, one is very careful about doing anything which may hurt another person. Not because of the quarrels that may ensue; that is not the problem. The problem is rather: "I feel that if I hurt him I am hurting myself." This is a very important sign. The other is that the mind begins to become quieter and does not generally get agitated over insignificant matters. This is in the beginning. In the later stages, even if the roof falls down, there is no reaction from the person. This is not due to callousness.

Please note that there is a difference between being callous about something and not being affected by it. The greatest of the *yogis* who were the *rishis* of ancient times—in recent times we had people like Swami Vivekananda—were not callous or lazy. They worked very hard but it was for some ideal; not for themselves. There were many difficulties, they faced many obstacles, but they generally remained unruffled. The result was that they continued to retain their equilibrium and the work was done smoothly. These are some of the signs a seeker may look for in the beginning. But, as he goes deeper into his *sadhana*, he will begin to discover newer dimensions even in relationships with other people.

***Q.2.** Will such a person manifest any qualitative difference externally and will he translate the change through his actions?*

M: There are external differences. There is no hard and fast rule regarding how this is translated into action. But the first thing I said is the criterion, viz., that the aspirant will be less self-centred than he was earlier. This is a clear indication of progress. As long as he has kindness and compassion in his heart, this change will take place in him. And if a person has actually realised the Self and is free, then his obligations do not have a hold on him. He may fulfil his obligations if he wants to. Nobody can force him to do anything he does not want to do.

***Q.3.** Can everyone achieve progress on the spiritual path? Also, why is not everyone drawn towards this path?*

M: Yes, it can be achieved by effort. But the guidance of a person who has already gone through it will be most helpful in this regard. As for some people not being interested in spirituality, there are many people who, for instance, are not interested in scientific investigations. They are only interested in day-to-day activities. They don't want to take interest in anything more complicated because their brains are not developed enough. There is a metaphysical explanation for this: Their subtle bodies and their *prarabhda karmas* or the *karmas* of their past lives have not matured. This is a debatable explanation which is only theoretical at present. What I am trying to say is that their brains are not developed enough to handle subtle issues. They are interested only in the world and what is happening in the world.

Q.4. *What is nididhyasana and how does it help in the quest for the Self?*

M: *Nididhyasana* is assimilating what you have learnt in your search for the Self. The subject is so subtle that listening to a talk or reading something once may not be enough. One will have to go into the subject again and again. After such repeated efforts, one may finally get an idea about what it is all about. In such matters, one has to understand quietly, deeply. This process is meditation. If you spend your entire life on *shravana* or listening to such subjects, then *manana* or thinking about the ideas and *nididhyasana* or understanding the subtle concepts will take place automatically. These are only different terms used for different parts of the same process. If you concentrate on one, the other stages will occur automatically. The only thing is that one must concentrate **fully**; not half-heartedly.

Q.5. *Can an agnostic achieve Self-realisation?*

M: Sure. But when he becomes Self-realised, he will no longer remain an agnostic. That is the point. In Vedantic enquiry unlike in *Bhakti*—I want to emphasise that I am not trying to grade these two paths in any way—one need not necessarily start one's enquiry with a premise that one has faith. The student could even begin by saying, "Yes, I have a doubt. So, let me find out what is true." Such a student is encouraged by his guru to approach the subject fearlessly. Since the doubts have entered his mind, the answers have also to be ascertained only by the same mind. Therefore, one can be an agnostic and still continue his enquiry till he achieves Self-realisation. But he should always begin his enquiry in the right manner. He should **suspend his judgement** till he is sure that he has reached the right conclusions. He need not believe everything that his guru tells him. At the same time, he should not begin his enquiry with the attitude that he **will not believe** anything that his guru tells him. It is important that the agnostic should have an open mind. If he does not find the Truth even after enquiring into things deeply, he will continue to be an agnostic. However, if he does succeed in his attempt, his belief will be all the stronger. 'Believe' and 'find out' have entirely contrary meanings. Belief implies that one doesn't know; so, one believes. When the agnostic tries to find out and comes to know the truth, there is no question of belief because he **just knows**.

Notes and References

1. The Absolute Truth is not revealed merely through introspection or contemplation, which is but subjective. According to Sri Shankara, it is revealed without the effort of the seeker (i.e., he cannot force it to occur)—*Purusha prayatnam vina prakati-bhuthah*. Though the Seer experiences it, he experiences it as an independent reality that is beyond his subjective consciousness.
2. Note: *Triguna—Sattva, Rajas and Tamas.*

7

IN THE WORLD BUT NOT OF THE WORLD

A question often asked is whether one can lead a spiritual life and at the same time be a householder earning wages, engaging in business, or being part of society and so on. The answer is an emphatic yes. To be spiritual you don't have to run away from the world. If you are careful and know what to do, you could reap the best of both worlds, God willing.

Many of you know of the simile of the lotus that grows in and derives its nourishment from water and yet doesn't let water wet its petals. Water can't stay on the petals of the lotus; it rolls off as droplets. That's the kind of life that a *yogi* lives. He draws sustenance for his body from the material world, but stays uncorrupted or undefiled by and unattached to it.

The inimitable Sri Ramakrishna Paramahamsa compares a *yogi* to a housemaid: "The housemaid treats the house she works in as if it were her own. She keeps everything clean and in order. She refers to the children of the household as her own, calling them 'my Radha', 'my Babu' and so on. But, in her heart of hearts, she knows that nothing belongs to her." That is the attitude of the true *yogi*. He lives and works in the world, lives with his family, his wife, children, friends, parents and so on, but knows through deep meditation that all this is temporary. He will have to leave all this some day. The only reality is the Self that is present everywhere and which shines in the deep recesses of his heart.

In the *Brihadaranyaka Upanishad*, Yajnavalkya declared to Mythreyi, his wife, "Listen, O! Mythreyi, the son is dear to the father, or the husband to the wife, not because of the son, or the father, or the husband, or the wife, but, because of the Self that is in them. Out of love for the Self which is in them one loves them, mistakenly thinking that the love is for the external form."

All human beings seek happiness. But, under the influence of ignorance, *avidya*, they seek for it in the external world of the senses. They enjoy a little bit, then lose it, and crave for more, while the real bliss, the permanent joy, a million times more blissful than the short-lived joys of the sensory world, is right there in the centre of their being. In the hearts of all human beings is the *Atman*, the reservoir for universal bliss and being.

Kabirdas illustrated this tragedy of man very well with the analogy of the musk-deer, which catches the odour of musk when the wind blows and searches for the source in the thorny bushes until its snout begins to bleed, not realising that the musk is right there in a pouch under its own tail.

All that may be true but you say that you can't live in the world and yet be unattached. Your mother, your father, your wife, your children all care for you. They are so attached to you, how can you then remain unattached? What is overlooked here is that nobody cares that much for anybody else unless the link is spiritual, like that of a true master and true disciple. No one, for instance, would like to take your place and go instead of you when death strikes. This is the ultimate test.

This does not mean that one should run away from the world and climb mountains or live in a forest, or become a *sannyasin*. *Sannyasa*, certainly, is a great stage of life, and some say even the greatest. True. Yet, can everyone become a *sannyasin*? How many true *sannyasins* can you find in these days? Are all people who wear ochre robes *sannyasins*? Many wear the robe as a means of earning a living. Many become *sannyasins* on the spur of the moment, and regret their rashness throughout their lives. They don't have the courage to give it up, throw out their hypocrisy. There are others who merely wear the robe and live a more sensuous life than even the ordinary householder. Rarely do we find a true *sannyasin*, a diamond in the dung-heap.

The ancients knew that it was not possible for most people to become renunciants without going through the experience of a householder. Therefore, they divided life into the four *ashramas* or stages. The celibate young man who pursued his studies of the scriptures as well as secular science and arts, was called the *brahmacharin*. A bachelor, he could pursue knowledge without hindrance or cares of the household. When he had completed his studies, he was to choose between a life of total renunciation, which he could adopt and was preeminently qualified for, and a householder's life.

Under most circumstances, he was advised to take up the householder's life, known as the *grihasthashrama*. To be a householder didn't mean to lead a permissive and generally licentious life. A householder was a most respected person. He was a married man with children who earned his living by honest means, looked after the family, conducted his daily spiritual duties, such as meditation, study of the scriptures, etc., and above all, contributed to the spiritual heritage, by providing food, cloth and shelter to the wandering mendicants, *sannyasins* and *sadhus*. Charity was part of his duty.

After his children had grown up and needed no support from him, he and his wife, who would also be proficient in spiritual matters, would seek quiet spots in and around forests, build a cool thatched hermitage and settle down to a life of tranquil contemplation and deeper study of the *Upanishads*. That was the stage of *vanaprastha*. When the *vanaprastha*, after proper investigation and deep meditation, became qualified to enter the blissful Supreme Consciousness and was convinced by his personal experience of the unreality of the external world when compared to the eternal *Brahman*, he was free to take *sannyas*. He then became a renunciant, who was above caste, creed or even sex, a free being with no position whatsoever, eating what chance brought him and sleeping under the trees or under the bare sky, his heart overflowing with the bliss of *Brahman*. He was a true *sanyasin*. Having experienced the world of senses, he had deliberately rejected it in favour of the Infinite—endless existence, consciousness, bliss *(sat, chit, ananda)*.

This traditional division of life into stages is all the more relevant today, although, this kind of *sannyas* is now difficult. Where are the householders who willingly support *sannyasins*? There may only be a very few! So many frauds have worn the ochre, that the ordinary man in the street is likely to abuse even a genuine *sannyasin* who begs for his food. And they are of course justified. Nobody loves to be taken for a ride.

For the *sannnyasin* who is part of an established *ashram*, it is a different matter. He does not have to beg for his food or clothes or to look for shelter. But he is not a *sannyasin* in the strictest sense of the term. He has left his family and entered a larger family, which is the organisation he belongs to. He doesn't work like the ordinary layman, but work he certainly does—in the ashram bookshop, in the temple, in the kitchen, keeping accounts, or in whatever area that needs his help in running the *ashram*. He seeks donations for the *ashram*, sells books, collects money for various *thithi pujas* that take place and so on. All that is not for himself but for the *ashram*, the existence of which is linked to his survival. If the *ashram* survives, he survives and vice versa.

Such *sannyasins* who belong to religious organisations also have a part to play in the drama of life.

And it is indeed an important part, but only if they can keep their hearts anchored to the Spirit and not get lost in organisational politics or the subtle desire to get their feet touched by devotees or the temptation to become famous orators or the arrogance of being spiritual advisers to important politicians.

For most people, married or unmarried, the best course advisable is to live in this wonderful creation of *maya*, and at the same time, keep in touch with the mighty Spirit who wields this magic wheel. The great *rishis* have done it—Vyasa, Yajnavalkya, so many others—great *yogis* like Lahiri Mahasay, the Sufi Masters, the great Ramakrishna Paramahamsa, although he is incomparable and in a class by himself. In the beginning, it is difficult to live like them, but by the guru's grace and sincere effort, you will find that even your day-to-day activities are performed more perfectly than before once the stream of *Atmic* bliss begins to flow through your heart for twenty-four hours of the day. You will become not only more loving, compassionate and tranquil but also more efficient, alert and practical.

Spirituality has nothing at all to do with callousness or lethargy. A lazy fellow who daydreams and does nothing useful should not be mistaken for a saint. People have this fear; they say, "If I get absorbed in *Brahman* what will happen to my work?" This is merely an excuse invented by the mind to prevent you from moving in the right direction. First of all, the man who is a serious seeker, seeks the Supreme Reality seriously, not caring for the consequences. What happens to the performance of daily duties is not his concern. However, he realises after studying the lives of great Self-realised beings who lived in the past, that, far from being or becoming inert or inactive, great sages, after realising the Supreme Reality, had always performed their functions much more efficiently and had done such marvellous work that ordinary mortals were astounded.

The fact is that such persons are not single-handed. They are million-handed, for the infinite *Brahman* works through them. Consider the examples of the great Sankaracharya, for instance, or more recently, the mighty Swami Vivekananda. Kabirdas worked on his loom while he sang his divine songs. Then there was the great King Janaka, a king who ruled his kingdom so well and yet was absorbed in *Brahman*. In the forest on the outskirts of Videha, the *rishi* Yajnavalkya used to give spiritual discourses and conduct dialogues on the Reality. The seat in the front row was always reserved for Janaka. Some of the *sannyasis* and recluses who lived in the forest thought that Yajnavalkya was swayed by the power of the throne for this prejudicial distinction. Sometimes they even expressed their misgivings. Yajnavalkya didn't attempt to answer them. One day, a messenger came gasping for breath and shouted that Janaka's palace in Videha was on fire and that the fire was spreading to the nearby forest. Many of the hermits immediately sprang up and ran to save their few belongings, while Janaka sat unperturbed and steady on his seat waiting for his teacher to continue his discourse. "This," said Yajnavalkya to the so-called pursuers of Truth, "is the difference between you and Janaka. He is the king and lives in a palace but is totally unattached to it. His mind is anchored in *Brahman*. You are hermits, yet your mind is always anchored to the few trinkets in your huts."

Janaka was called *Rajarishi*. You will find Krishna referring to *Rajarishis* in the fourth chapter of the *Bhagavad Gita,* called *Jnana Karma Sannyasa Yoga*. In verse 1 he says: "I imparted this immortal yoga to Vivaswan, Vivaswan imparted it to Manu, and Manu to Ikshwaku'. In verse 2: "This yoga, handed down from teacher to disciple in succession, was known to the *Rajarishis*. But owing to the long lapse of time it was lost to the world." In verse 3: "I have today disclosed to you the same ancient yoga, which is a noble secret, for you are my devotee and friend."

It is this yoga of *nishkamyakarma* that is ideal for this age of *Kali*. *Nishkamyakarma* or desireless action does not mean that you just keep on working like an automaton, no matter what the results are. You certainly set yourself a target to achieve and you plan well to achieve it by putting in hard work with single-pointed attention. This ability to concentrate will come with the practice of meditation. But the difference is that, unlike the ordinary man, you will not be shattered if the results are not as expected. In gain or loss, your mind will be balanced, steady, and unperturbed, and therefore, fully equipped to deal with the situation or to make alternate plans. This *nishkamyakarma* is also applied to meditation. The practice of *dhyana* is continued calmly, whether the results are good or imperfect during any particular session. Soon, the mind attains a certain tranquillity and becomes fit to receive the experience known as *samadhi*.

So, a spiritual life is not incompatible with worldly existence. Actually, a properly lived life in the world is conducive to meditation. This is especially true, if you are also inclined to practise *asanas*, *pranayam*, etc., as laid down in the path of *ashtanga yoga*. A wandering *sannyasin* cannot get proper diet, rest, bath, etc., prescribed for such yoga. The *Gita* puts it in a nutshell by saying, "This yoga is not for one who eats too much, or too little, sleeps too much, or too little." Moderation is the key word for the *hatayogi* and the *rajayogi*. And this is best provided in a householder's life.

For a start, occasional retreats to quiet and conducive places away from the bustle of the marketplace are necessary for the practice of meditation. Sri Ramakrishna used to say that, when the plants are small, a fence of thorns around them is necessary to prevent cows and goats from eating them. But, once a tree has grown up a little, the fences are no longer needed. Once you are established in meditation with your master's grace and guidance, you can live right in the middle of the marketplace and still be established in *Brahman*.

Advocating the life of a householder does not entail a *laissez-aller*—an unrestrained freedom to live as you will. You cannot rob, cheat, lie or do any heinous action to harass others and still attain a spiritual state. Yet, the moment the desire to reach a spiritual state is awakened, a person's psyche begins to change. However despicable a person is, his yearning for the Divine increases, he begins to practise his *sadhana* more and more diligently and anything that is not conducive to spiritual life falls off by itself. If he has been following a life that is sinful till then, in the sense that it is against his spiritual principles, the Great Beings who govern the universe, in their infinite kindness, take him out of it and bring him into a profession that is compatible with the spiritual way of life. There is nothing to worry. Greater forces exist, which can change your attitude and way of life so that you pursue the path without hindrance, and yet, are well provided for materially; not only you, but also your dependants.

If you have seen spiritual giants leading a simple life with minimum necessities, it is because they are in a supreme state of bliss and have voluntarily discarded material comforts. What do they lose? They have gained the Universal Spirit. Of what use are mere trinkets to them? But, it is not a rule that God-realised souls should live in poverty. Some have lived in the midst of luxury, yet unattached to it, and performing their duties efficiently. Some others have been householders, having a large number of dependants to look after. After realising that everything in the universe is the Supreme Lord himself, great *Vignanis* have made the whole universe their family in place of the tiny little family that they had renounced and then lead a life of constant service. For example, Valmiki the dacoit, became Valmiki the *rishi*. The main thing is the intense desire to realise the Divine and the necessary discipline to practise *sadhana*. It does not matter who you are or what you are as long as your desire is strong and your *sadhana* is earnest.

I must tell about a great *yogi* I met in Dehradun. My Master directed me to him to learn more about the *kundalini*. I knew that he was a big businessman but I was startled at my first sight of him. I even wondered if I had not come to the wrong person! He met me at the Dehradun railway station, a tall, clean-shaven, middle-aged man in a three-piece suit. Outside, he escorted me to his Mercedes-Benz car, complete with a uniformed chauffeur. I was tired and slept almost all the way up to Delhi. He put me up at an upmarket second floor flat in Greater Kailash in New Delhi, not far from his bungalow, where he lived with his wife, three children, and three Alsatians. He told me that his chief business was real estate. But, he was truly a highly advanced *yogi* as I discovered in a few days. Not only did he enlighten me theoretically on the *kundalini* and the *Srividya*, he also demonstrated things practically when the need arose. Unfortunately, he was one of those who preferred to remain unknown for certain reasons of his own, and therefore, I cannot reveal his identity.

Now, after all this, if a rare soul among you still feels that he is qualified to lead a *sanyasin's* life, think seriously, deeply. As a *Vaishnavite sadhu*, who then lived a little beyond Vasishta Guha, near Rishikesh cautioned me, "*Sanyasa* is a high state, and few are qualified for it. You have to climb many steps to reach the top and, if you by chance slip and fall from such a great height, you might get seriously injured and may not find it easy to recover." Do sit quietly and take stock and, if you still want to, go ahead. But, let not the *sanyasa* be like the one Sri Ramakrishna referred to when discouraging certain people from becoming renunciants. He said, "Suddenly you are filled with a desire for renunciation, or so you believe. Telling no one, you rush off to Benaras. A few days later, you write home, saying that you are well and are looking for a good job and nobody need worry."

Many people wonder how to conduct their daily business of living while practising *sadhana*. For example, one may wonder, how a man dedicated to a spiritual life of non-violence, peace and goodwill, can scold or take to task his employees if he errs. Doesn't getting angry, shouting at someone and so on retard spiritual progress? Listen to this story. Once, there lived a huge cobra, so dangerous that no one dared to walk across the path besides which was his hole. One day, a young *brahmachari* on pilgrimage had to cross that village. All the people warned him not to go along the dreaded path because the cobra was sure to kill him. The *Brahmin* told them not to worry because he knew enough charms to keep the snake at bay. As he approached the snake's hole, he saw the cobra with its hood raised, ready to strike. He tamed him with his *mantras* and the snake became his disciple. He taught the snake the elements of spiritual practice. He also told the snake that, if he wanted to lead a spiritual life, he had to give up biting people. The snake agreed.

On his way back after a year, the *brahmachari* stopped at the same village. He saw that the street where the snake lived was no longer deserted. People walked up and down fearlessly. He asked some street urchins about the snake. "Ah," they said, "he is still there in the hole. But, who cares for him any more; he has stopped biting. Even when we pelt him with stones he does not bite. So we finally broke his backbone. He is now an invalid and comes out with great difficulty only in the night for his food."

The *brahmachari* went to the hole and called out to his disciple softly. "Gurudev," said the snake in a feeble voice, for he was almost starved to death, "I am here. I followed your advice, and stopped biting and you can see for yourself what has happened to me. Anyway, I am continuing to meditate." "Oh, you poor unfortunate fellow!" said the *brahmachari*. "Why did you not use your common sense? I told you not to bite, but did I tell you not to hiss? All you had to do was to hiss and nobody would have dared approach you."

There is another illusion that some people have about spirituality. They think that by the practice of religion, you become soft-brained and walk around with your head in the clouds, incapable of even buying good vegetables from the market at a suitable price. On the contrary, nothing can be farther from the truth. The experienced *sadhak* knows not only how to get into a trance but also knows how to get out of it and attend to his daily life efficiently. He does not live as if in a daze. Also, if you see someone with a long face and pained expression, do not mistake it for an effect of religion. It is dyspepsia, not religion. Ask him to do something about his digestion. Perhaps, he suffers from constipation. A truly religious man always has a joyous countenance.

There is a telling anecdote about Swami Vivekananda. A young man once went to him and said that he wanted to renounce the world and become a great being like Buddha. The Swami agreed that it was indeed a laudable idea and asked him how well educated he was, how much wealth or landed property he had, and what high status he enjoyed in society. He found the young man was zero in all these things. The Swami was furious. What on earth did the chap possess that he was going to renounce? He advised him to go and do a bit of honest labour first, earn a substantial sum of money, and then come back to him and tell him if he was prepared to renounce it.

Begin your *sadhana* now, ***this instant***; everything else will be taken care of. If the thought "I am such a simple man, how could I attain God?" occurs to you, remember that it is merely an excuse that a tricky mind puts forth to prevent you from following the right path. If you wait to become morally perfect before you begin your spiritual practices, that day will never come. Start today and, as the divine bliss enters your heart, you will get purified inside and outside. You will get the strength and inspiration to mould your life as you wish.

8

THE GAYATRI MANTRA

The *Gayatri Mantra* is one of the most ancient *mantras* of this country. It is said that whoever sings (chants) it is protected, *gayantam trayate, yasmat Gayatri tyabhidhiyate.* The importance of this *mantra* lies in the fact that it deals with the relation between man and the universe as well as the Reality behind both—it is concerned with the process of Self-realisation, the gradual unfolding of our essential nature, which is none other than the *Upanishadic Brahman.* Meditation on *Gayatri* leads one beyond the three states (already mentioned in the earlier chapters) to the stateless condition of *Turiya*, the Undivided Consciousness.

A natural question then is: "Is *Gayatri* only for the spiritual seeker and not for the man in the world involved in the pains and pleasures of daily living? The answer is an emphatic **NO**; for the uniqueness of *Gayatri* is in its universal application. It is as important to the spiritual seeker as to the practical householder. The importance becomes clear when we consider the fact that, not only is it as *Mahamantra* an indivisible element in all religious rituals, but it is also the *mantra* used for the daily *sandhyavandanam* (rite to be performed at dawn, dusk, and preferably at midday too) of the twice-born,[1] *Brahmin*, *Kshatriya* and *Vaishya*.

There is a reason for such a universal application.

Though caught up as we are in the 'everydayness' of living, we still need clear and sharp perception to comprehend the deeper significance of our mundane facts and problems if we are to face them effectively and practically. Intellect or reason is often incapable of providing us the desired clarity and the result is invariably an attitude of: 'The spirit is willing but the flesh is weak.' Let us look at the world around us. Is it lack of intellect or reasoning capacity that has taken us where we are? Certainly we do have knowledge on the superficial, surface level. How, otherwise, can one explain the aberrant behaviour of even some of our great philosophers? Or scientists? Or leaders? They constantly present a dichotomy in their lives; for example, a public persona of moral rectitude and a private life of moral turbidity. What is patent is that both the thinking man and the unthinking man in the street are the same when it comes to their basic attitude towards life; all suffer from the same malady—the lack of discrimination. And, discrimination, according to our scriptures, especially Vedanta, is only possible when a faculty higher than the intellect is employed. That faculty is *buddhi*, which can be loosely defined as intuition tempered with intellect. And *Gayatri* is the vehicle or mode to reach this source of discrimination or *viveka*. The development of discrimination through *buddhi* is essential, not only in preventing us from being *adharmic*, but in propelling us towards the ultimate enlightenment.

Let us now consider the word *gayatri*. *Gayatri* is actually the name of a particular form of Sanskrit *shloka* written in what is known as the *gayatri* meter. The *gayatri* meter consists of twenty-four syllables, *aksharas*, evenly distributed in its three *padas*, feet. Hence it is also known as *tripada gayatri*. (There are other meters which contain twenty-four syllables but their distribution is not as in the *Gayatri*.) There are other *gayatri mantras* also (see footnote 1); for example, the first *vedic mantra* itself is in *gayatri* meter. But the *Gayatri Mantra*, by virtue of its universal appeal, has appropriated for itself the name of the meter, so that any mention of this meter evokes the words of this *mantra*.

Each foot of the *Gayatri* represents the *Rig*, *Yajur*, and *Sama Vedas*. (The *Atharva Veda* has its own *Gayatri*.) In fact, it is mentioned in the *Vedas: Gayatrim chandasma mata*. *Chandasma* here means the *Vedas* and, therefore, *Gayatri* is the mother of all the *Vedas*.)

Let us look at the *mantra* itself:

Aum Bhur Bhuvah Suvaha
Tat Savitur Varenyam
Bhargo Devasya Dheemahi
Dhiyo Yonah Prachodayat.

If you scan these lines, you will notice that the first line does not conform to the *gayatri* meter. It consists of the *pranava*, *Aum*, and *maha vyahritis*, the seven spheres of existence, beginning with the physical, *bhuloka*[2], forming the first part of the *mantra*. The second part consists of the next two lines ending in *dheemahi*, it being metrically divided into two lines. The third part is the last line.

This division into parts is not arbitrary; it represents the three stages of one's unfoldment towards the Ultimate Consciousness. The first part prepares the spiritual background for the operation of the second and third parts. While the first makes the aspirant the *upadhi*, the right vehicle or receptacle, for the descent of the Supreme Consciousness, the second part intensifies his mental aspiration for it. But the attainment of the Ultimate Consciousness can only be through Divine Grace and this Grace is obtained through the self-surrender of the third part.

In order to understand the significance of the *mantra*, an analysis of its main elements is necessary, starting with the *pranava*.

The word *AUM* is a threefold word, although when vocalised, it is a single sound. It can be divided into three sections: 'a', 'u', and 'm'. The *Upanishads* and *Vedas* have given various meanings to these three sounds. One of the frequently encountered interpretations is that 'a' represents creation, 'u' preservation, and 'm' destruction or the transformation of something old into something new. The last can only happen by starting afresh with 'a'. Even the manner in which the letters have been arranged is significant—of course, in the production of the sound *AUM*, the letters are coalesced. 'A' is the most easily produceable sound and is known in Sanskrit as *akara*. It is, in Sanskrit as in most languages of the world, the first letter of the alphabet. The next sound 'u' has to be rolled out from inside the mouth and over the tongue—by the nature of its production, its utterance can be extended or maintained for a longer period—and it represents the middle state of preservation. The sound 'm' can only be made by closing the lips and it means the last stage of a full cycle. To produce a new sound, the mouth has to be opened again. That is, 'm' symbolically brings to an end what the mouth began with.

Apart from this symbolic, physiological representation, *Aum* has various other interpretations. In one, 'a' stands for *sattva* and *Brahma*, 'u' for *rajas* and *Vishnu*, and 'm' for *tamas* and *Shiva*; this again is a modification of the earlier one. Another interpretation is that 'a' is *akar* or form, the earth element; 'u' is the upward moving air element, and 'm' is the void.

Of all the interpretations, the one that has the highest philosophical import is mentioned in the *Chandogya Upanishad*, and in greater detail, in the *Mandukya Upanishad*. The *Mandukya* says that 'a' is our waking state, wherein we normally recognise the world using our senses and mind. We live in the world and enjoy and suffer as we undergo different experiences. As a state of consciousness, as mentioned elsewhere, it is the *jagrata awastha*. It entails, therefore, that 'u' used in this *mantra* represents the dream state or *swapna awastha* and the *sukshma sharira*, the subtle body. Finally, 'm' represents *sushupti*, the deep sleep state or the *karana sharira,* the causal body. The utterance of *Aum* is not abrupt as in an angry snort. It leaves, as it were, a contrail of humming known as the *ardha matra*. This is similar to the sound which continues after a gong has been struck. This represents the *Turiya awastha.*

By the letters of the English alphabet, one cannot capture the total essence of the meaning of *Aum*. In Devanagari, the word is written in a special manner. This is not the simplest manner in which it can be written in that script; the simplest representation for the sound would be.... But it is written symbolically with a characteristic flourish.... Like all the other things in Vedanta, this particular symbol is designed in such a way that one distinguishes the subtle from the gross. The form of the sound aids in visualising the different states of consciousness in conjunction with the vibrations caused by the chant. (Lengthening the 'u' sound while chanting is supposed to transfer the effect of the chanting to everyone, while lengthening the sound of the 'm' is good for one's own getting into a meditative mood.) As written in Devanagari, the upper bend of the character stands for the *bhur* and *jagratawastha*, the lower bend for the *bhuvar* and *swapnawastha*. The other bend, which is like an elephant's trunk, represents the *suvarloka* and *sushupti*. (Lord Ganesha is called *Aumkararupa* for the reason that *Aum* in Devanagari is more like the ideograph of the face of an elephant.) The small crescent moon with a star on top is the *ardha matra*, the reverberatory or resonant sound that continues after completing the utterance of *Aum*. This is also called the *anahata chakra*. *Anahata* means that which is not struck and, therefore, it denotes an unstruck sound. In meditation, one is supposed to hear this sound internally.

Since an exposition on *Aum* can be endless and, therefore, beyond the scope of this short essay, only one final reference need be made as to its importance by turning to the *Katha Upanishad*: (*Yama* tells *Nachiketas*): That word which all the *vedas* declare, which all the austerities proclaim, desiring which people live the life of a religious student, that word to thee I shall tell in brief. That is *AUM*. This syllable is verily the everlasting spirit. This syllable, indeed, is the highest end; knowing this very syllable, whatever anyone desires will, indeed, be his.[3]

The next three words of the first line—*Bhur*, *Bhuvar* and *Suvar*—are, in a way, further explanation of the symbolic content of *Aum*. However, there is a slight difference; where *pranava* is directed towards the *Ishvara* as Indivisible Consciousness, the *vyahritis* point to the deities that rule the physical, astral and mental planes of our ordinary life. These deities are *Agni*, *Vayu*, and *Aditya* and the three *vyahritis* are the *bija*, seed *mantras* of the respective divinities.

There is a further affinity between the *pranava* and the *vyahritis*. According to the *Chandogya Upanishad*, Prajapati meditated on the threefold knowledge (the three *Vedas*) and, from the result of the meditation, extracted its essence, namely *Bhuh* from the *Rig*, *bhuvah* from the *Yajur* and *Suvah* from the *Sama Veda*. When he further brooded on these *vyahritis*, the syllable *Aum* was the result.

Coming to the *mantra* proper, it ought to be pointed out—and this is very important—that the *Gayatri* is translated in as many ways as there are scholars with their individual views. Many reasons can be given for such diversion of views. Leaving alone the incompetence of some of the interpreters, we may arrive at one reason for the variants; the extremely rich and complex nature of the Sanskrit language. Often, the same word or expression has different meanings in different contexts. Or, it can have several cognate meanings in the same context. Closely allied to this, is the highly inflected nature of the knowledge which determines its syntax. A strict adherence to grammatical analysis will yield a sort of meaning but not the right one. The only correct interpretation depends on the apprehension of the subtle context which is beyond the rational linguistic deciphering.[4] In short, any true meaning that can be arrived at can only be through the *buddhi*, which faculty the *mantra* is aiming at developing in the aspirant. Such a situation may appear like a *petitio principi*, an argument in circles. Yet, therein lies the *mantra's* power-the power to draw the aspirant closer and closer to the contemplation of the words of the *mantra*.

A rough literal interpretation, as different from translation of the *mantra* is as follows: "We contemplate upon the Originator or Source of everything, that adorable, effulgent Divinity, and pray that our intelligence may be illumined and stimulated, so that we would be enabled to understand the Absolute Truth."

There is one crucial word in this *mantra* which sets it apart from all other *mantras*. It is the word *dheemahi*. It means either 'We meditate upon' or 'May we meditate upon'. Whatever meaning we select—an assertion or prayer—the important aspect is the plural form of the word. And this has great significance. Since it is a *mantra* to be chanted, generally as a personal *mantra*, why should it have the plural subject? The plural implies that the prayer is for the benefit of all, though the aspirant is seeking the development of spiritual consciousness. The 'we' underlines the same latent Universal Consciousness in all. It is this transcendence over a desire for narrow personal benefit that imbues the *Gayatri Mantra* with its great power.

As with all *mantras*, *Gayatri* also has its tutelary deity, though it is addressed to *Savita*, the sun. And that deity is *Gayatri* who is the female counterpart of the trinity: *Brahma*, *Vishnu*, and *Shiva*, or more appropriately, their consorts *Saraswati*, *Lakshmi* and *Kali* representing learning, wealth, and protection. They are prayed to for personal worldly boons, while *Gayatri* is invoked to give us the *buddhi* to understand our true nature, knowing which we have everything. It is our identification with our individual selves that flings us into bondage. But the divine light of *Savita* helps us to free ourselves from our bondage, so that the power of *Gayatri* envelops us.

Above all, the *Gayatri Mantra* is unique in another way. It is the only *mantra* which is the combination of a prayer and a *mantra*—it combines the inherent power of the sound of a *mantra* (which sometimes has no meaning for the chanter) with the power of the prayer.

Notes and References

1. Exclusion of the fourth caste, *varna*, and women from reciting *Gayatri* may be subject to controversy and this cannot be resolved within the ambit of the present essay; the *raison d'etre* for the *varnashrama* is likely to generate more heat than light and no debate on it has ever been conclusive. However, it may be pointed out, as an aside, that there are other *Gayatri Mantras* like *Vishnu Gayatri*, *Shiva Gayatri*, *Hanuman Gayatri*, etc., which are not restricted by caste and gender.
2. *Note:* Generally, a *mantra* is associated with a particular deity, e.g., *Shiva-pancakshari* with the name of the deity, Shiva, and the metrical form (distribution of syllables in an order that decides the sound and tone of the *mantra*) together synergises the effects; the *mantra* can be chanted without knowing the meaning of it and one can still benefit from it.
3. As translated by Dr Radhakrishnan.
4. It is very interesting to compare this situation to that of the modern philosophy of Deconstruction. Deconstruction was initiated by the French philosopher,

Jacques Derrid, in the late 1960's, who claimed that Western philosophy had become rooted in a tradition which sought truth and certainty of meaning by privileging certain types of interpretation and repressing others; he emphasised, on the other hand, the instability and deferral of meaning in language and the limitlessness (or impossibility) of interpretation—*Oxford English Reference Dictionary*.

9

MISCONCEPTIONS ABOUT KUNDALINI

Kundalini is a word that has fascinated thousands of people. Most people who have only a rudimentary knowledge of yoga or mysticism talk of *kundalini* and what fantastic and sometimes downright silly ideas come out!

Kundalini seems to be the most misunderstood of terms. Some think that it is a mysterious force linked to black magic and the orgies of *Kapalic tantrics*. Others, well educated in matters of human anatomy and physiology but, who unfortunately have not studied either the relevant texts or have not been guided by a spiritual teacher, proclaim that it is nothing but a nerve, right vagus nerve for instance. There are others who say that the *kundalini* and the centres through which it moves are all on the astral or some such plane and even paint it in fantastic technicolours, which they consider as better than the diagrammatic representation of the *chakras*.

A handful of people who have written on the subject like Sir John Woodroff, the author of 'Serpent Power', have really taken the trouble to go into the subject, theoretically and practically, and therefore, provide a wealth of information. There are others, great sages and yogis, who have had true personal experience of *kundalini* but, for various reasons, hesitate to put anything in writing.

The traditional texts that deal with the *kundalini,* like the *Hatayoga Pratheepika, Satchakra Nirupanam,* the *Tantras,* including various commentaries on *Soundarya Lahiri* and the writings of Bhaskara Raya, Kaivalyashrama, and Lakshmidhara, need the guidance of an initiated guru to yield their secrets. Such gurus are indeed rare nowadays.

There is nothing to wonder, therefore, at the rather ridiculous spectacle of thousands of people sitting with closed eyes, expecting the self-appointed guru to arouse the *kundalini* en masse for everyone at once.

There are people who claim that their *kundalini* was definitely raised, because they felt a tickling sensation in their palms. A hypnotist can do better; he can make you feel a tickling sensation in the neck or any other part of the body that you name.

"Why not?" ask the votaries of the instant enlightenment cult. "Ramakrishna Paramahansa enlightened Swami Vivekananda by a single touch; Nityananda Avadhuta awakened Swami Muktananda's *kundalini* by a mere glance! *Shaktipath* is possible. Ancient texts declare it." But *Shaktipath* is not something you can buy off the shelf — it is not a marketable commodity.

Just reflect a little and do not fall into a trap. Why did Sri Ramakrishna choose only Swami Vivekananda to receive that special touch? So also with the great Nityananda. A flower seller at Ganeshpuri, who hasn't progressed much spiritually to this day, was a protege of Sri Nityananda. Why hasn't he been granted *Shaktipath*?

It is true that Masters of high spiritual stature can awaken the *kundalini* or spiritual consciousness in an individual by their mere wish. But then, they do so only for the disciple with the right qualifications, intense longing for the Truth, and only for one who does intense *sadhana*. When the disciple is ripe, the guru seeks him out to bestow his grace. So, be cautious when someone offers spiritual enlightenment wholesale.

We shall not go into the many details regarding the number of petals of the given *chakra*, the colour, etc. Such details are not important. And those who are interested can find them in the Sanskrit originals or in the excellent translations available, like Sir John Woodroff's *Serpent Power*. But regarding the *Hatayogic* and other practices found in books, one should not resort to practising them without the guidance of an experienced teacher. Not only are they useless without such guidance but are downright dangerous.

There are instances of unfortunate enthusiasts who have gone mad practising what they thought to be spriritual exercises. This is apart from the physical ailments that can be caused by the improper practice of *Hatayogic* postures and breathing exerìcises called *pranayama*.

Now to the bare essentials of *kundalini* yoga. The *kundalini* is a spiritual force or energy, symbolised by a serpent, which remains sleeping or inactive in a potential stage like a coiled spring in all human beings, male or female, at the extreme lower end of the spine in a centre called *muladhara chakra*. A *yogi* is different from the ordinary human being in that he, by controliling the sexual impulse intimately linked with the *kundalini*, and by practice of spiritual exercises taught by his guru, manages to arouse the *kundalini* serpent from its sleep and guides it upwards step by step along the central *sushumna* channel in the spine until it reaches the *sahasrara chakra* or the *sahasrara padma*, the thousand-petalled lotus situated in the head.

In all human beings, the *prana*, or the lifeforce, moves and performs its functions through two *nadis* or paths, called the *pingala* on the right side of the spine and the *ida* on the left. The *pingala,* also called 'ha' in *Hatayoga,* is the positive chanìnel and the *ida,* also called 'tha', is the negative. The central nadi, on both sides of which are the *ida* and the *pingala,* is called the *sushumna* and lies in the core of the spinal chord. The sushumna channel is closed normally, and the *yogi* opens it up by his practice, brings the negative and positive *pranas* together at the base of the spine through *pranayama* and, striking the *kundalini,* wakes her up and takes her up along the cleared central *sushumna.* As the *kundalini* moves upwards from the *muladhara,* it passes through five other centres, situated one above the other, called *swadhistana,* a little above the reproductive organs, *manipura* in the navel, *anahata* in the middle of the chest, *vishuddha* in the throat and *aajnya* in the space between the eyebrows before it reaches the seventh centre in the brain. The very awakening of the *kundalini* in the *muladhara* is accompanied by blissful sensations in that centre. As it rises and moves through each *chakra,* described aptly as lotuses with petals drooping down, they straighten up and bloom at its magic touch. Not only does the bliss experienced by the yogi reach unimaginable heights, but also his eyes are opened to greater vistas, wonderful realms, which he never before could have imagined existed. His physical body as well as his subtle body, mind, and intellect become refined and yogic powers like clairvoyance, etc., begin to appear spontaneously.

When the *kundalini* reaches the *sahasrara,* it being the *Sakthi,* unites with Shiva, the passive principle, and they become undifferentiated in one vast ocean of peace and omnipresent being. The *yogi,* lost in that state, is said to be in *samadhi.* When the *kundalini* descends again to the lower centres, the *yogi* is conscious of the world but he is now a new person. The alchemist's stone has touched him and he has been transmuted into gold. He may put on an armour of base metals to join the battle of life, but inside, is pure gold. Of course, he can lead the *kundalini* again to meet the Lord at will. Such a *yogi* is verily a manifestation of Shiva, Shivam, auspiciousness and Shivoham; Shivoham is his *mantrasiddhi*.

Here, we will not go into the controversy which goes on all the while about whether it is physical or whether it is psycho-physical energy and so on. We will also not go into the debate regarding the *chakras* being actual nerve plexuses or purely astral formations. These we can leave to those who have time for such things. It will certainly be useful to discover the truth about these facts, but this is a question of priorities. Our priorities are different.

Suffice it to say, that there is certainly a link between the *kundalini* and the physical body and it works both ways. Firstly, certain physical postures and exercises, including breath control, and practices that alter the chemistry of the body, like fasting, etc., do accelerate and induce arousal of the *kundalini,* provided the other essentials are there. Secondly, sex is intimately linked with the *kundalini.* The control and sublimation of sex is one of the chief requisites for the arousal of the *kundalini.* Apart from the spiritual and psychic developments that it brings about, it also effects biological changes in the physical organism which can be clearly felt by the *yogi. kundalini* is none other than the Parashakti, the Supreme Energy, which, after having performed its creation in the macrocosm as well as in the microcosm, rests in the *muladhara.* It doesn't mean that it is only a spent force — the leftover part — of the Supreme Energy that is involved in the creation and remaining at the *muladhara.* On the contrary, the *kundalini* is potentially the same Omnipotent Power by which the whole universe is manifested and by which it functions.

The following invocatory *shloka* of the *Isavasya Upanishad* underlines the infinite, indestructible, immutable nature of that Energy:

Om purnamadaha purnamidam
purnat purnamudachyate
Purnasya purnamadaya
purnamevavisasyate
Om Shantih, Shantih, Shantih.

Loosely translated, this could be read as:

Infinite is the invisible; so is the visible.
The visible universe finds its expression in the Infinite
(Yet) the Infinite remains complete in spite of Its expression in the finite universe.
Om Peace! Peace! Peace!

10

FEAR OF DEATH

Undoubtedly, everyone fears death to a greater or lesser extent; unless, of course, one is a saint who is above the concern of life and death, or at the absurd extreme, one is suicide-prone. Is it because, in essence, there is something permanent in the human being and we are aware that it is only the impermanent body that is disappearing with death and not the Being which is supposed to be there and which does not disappear?

A positive answer to this question, to say the least, is debatable, for the reason that most people are not aware of the existence of something permanent apart from the body which forms the core of a human being. The normal man is not aware of this, and not being aware of it, there can be no reason that he would think in this manner. This is, of course, not to deny the possibility of entertaining such a thought. It is quite probable that, somewhere deep down, every human being feels that there must be something permanent somewhere and he therefore does not like to end his existence. Such a feeling only comes when you feel that everything is going to end and death is imminent. In such cases we are afraid of death because we do not know what is going to come after death.

However, on closer inspection, you will find that the fear of death is not because you don't know what is going to happen after death but is because you are afraid of losing everything that you have gathered during your lifetime. The greatest fear that we have is that we will lose everything that we possess, or rather everything that we think that we possess when we die. Nobody really possesses anything but the feeling is that we do. Hence, this fear is uppermost in the mind of a person who is about to die. We think that death is going to wipe the whole thing off. That is the main reason for the fear of death. Therefore, we would like to feel that there is some existence after death where we can possess something else. The mind can then be satisfied that if we lose something here, we get something over there. I am not discussing whether life exists after death or not; it is a moot point without any definitive conclusion. I am just saying that the fear of death is mainly because one is afraid of losing one's possessions, not only physical and material possessions, but all that one can think of. More than physical and material possessions, there are very many mental things that we create and stick to. Even these things will disappear.

For the existence of an imperishable, immutable substance behind the perishable and the changing as proclaimed by our scriptures—which could be viewed as not a projected wish to subdue our fear of death—the experience of Sri Ramana Maharshi may be adduced as a proof, again a proof not easily verifiable. He had a unique experience very early in his life in which he thought he was going to die. So, he said to himself (he was very young), "I am going to die. Let me lie down on the bed like a dead body." He had seen how dead bodies are laid out on the floor before they are taken away to the cremation ground. He then closed his eyes. There was no breathing; everything had stopped; there was absolutely no movement. But then he realised that he was still alive! This was not a mere simulation of death that anyone can resort to by the sheer power of an overactive imagination. He really had an experience of death in the sense that he had actually stopped breathing, there was no movement, and he could see everything that was happening down there. He said, "Now the body is dead; they are going to carry it to the cremation ground." When he discovered that he was not dead, he thought to himself, "I am still here but that is what death must be like. So, perhaps, there is something which survives after death. Is it physical, is it mental, or is it something beyond both the body and the mind? Is it just the brain that is trying to protect itself or is there an operator for the brain also, for the brain is a very complex computer?"

11

PAIN IN THE LIGHT OF YOGA

Nobody wants to experience pain unless one is gauranteed that, by experiencing the pain, more happiness will result. I don't mind going through some pain as long as some happiness arises due to this and I can blot my pain out. Otherwise, nobody wants to experience pain. This is because of the innate tendency of the mind to move towards happiness which is nothing but the easing of pain which manifests in everybody. Every human being has this tendency to move towards happiness. The only problem is that, if you watch out very carefully, you will see that, after every bit of happiness, some unhappiness again crops up. When you think that everything that contributed to your sorrow is over and that you are happy, something else happens and the happiness is again gone. Now the *rishis* declare that there is a core of happiness inside you. If you turn to this, what you do or don't achieve outside is absolutely of no account. Searching for this happiness, the mind looks outside, not knowing about its existence within. Therefore, whenever there is pain, it tries to get rid of that pain. To get rid of pain is itself happiness; one doesn't have to possess any other positive happiness. When pain is gone, there is happiness. The body always does not like to feel pain and a biological mechanism exists in it to protect it from pain. So, such automatic reactions to pain occur always. Who would like to be in pain? One tries to avoid pain as far as possible for the physical body as well as for the mind. When the body is sick, when there is pain in the body, then the mind cannot take off to anything subtler or higher, because it will always be thinking of the pain in the body. With exercise or posture, one has to make sure consciously not to cause pain as far as possible. That is why yoga does not involve any physical torture. Sitting upright is not torture. It is normally possible for everybody but, for the person who has not been trained from an early age, it may be difficult. If one starts early enough, one can sit straight and be very, very comfortable. But if one cannot sit straight, one's Self-realisation will not suffer because of that; this much I can assure. But it is good to sit straight. When you are sitting straight, you are alert and ready and you feel that you are under control. But if somebody has a back pain or some problem, it is terrible to tell that person, "Look, you must sit straight for spiritual enquiry; you can't lean on anything." So, let him lean on a pillow or whatever; it does not matter.